T0006083

A GUIDE TO
Midwestern Conversation

A GUIDE TO
Midwestern Conversation

Taylor Kay Phillips

Illustrations by Jovaney Hollingsworth

TEN SPEED PRESS
California | New York

For Mom, Dad, and Tess—
my favorite Midwestern conversationalists.

And for Felipe—
my home away from hometown.

Contents

Introduction

Well, hey there!

Come on in, sit down. Can I getcha anything? A coffee? Glass of wine? Bagel bites from the garage fridge? You sure? Okay, well, you just let me know.

Welcome to *A Guide to Midwestern Conversation*, a manual to and a road trip through the twelve states designated as "The Midwest" by the *Encyclopaedia Britannica*, *New World Encyclopedia*, United States Census Bureau, and most dads. Those states are, in alphabetical order (well, almost; I'm starting with my home state but, I promise, this is the only time I'll play favorites): Missouri, Illinois, Indiana, Iowa, Kansas, Michigan, Minnesota, Nebraska, North Dakota, Ohio, South Dakota, and Wisconsin.

I wanted to get that out of the way first, because sometimes people like to debate what "counts" as the Midwest, and to be honest with you, that whole conflict isn't really my thing.

While "The Midwest" is a certain defined geographical region (not debatable within this book), a "Midwesterner" can live, visit, and squeeze right past ya anywhere in the world! We're united by much more than the many (many!) acres of land that divide us. The similarities in the way we talk, give directions, and cover our necks during tornado drills bind us together almost as much as our love of puppy chow.

It's not really fair to call the Midwest "misunderstood" because (1) I think we Midwesterners understand our deal pretty gosh darn well, and (2) I don't think anyone else (ahem, Coasties) has tried hard enough to even get it wrong. But one thing that I think folks get a little bit twisted is the idea of "Midwestern Nice." Some people characterize it as being passive-aggressive, intimating that we're as mean as everyone else but we just do it with a smile. Negativity with a side of deep-fried disingenuousness, if you will. Others come down on the opposite side, claiming that Midwestern Nice is a form of superhuman kindness and hospitality. That we, as a species, are just so deeply *nice*, we are incapable of feeling anger or displeasure, let alone of expressing it.

Ope, surprise! It's neither. The truth, like us, is somewhere in the middle.

Midwestern conversation is a language all its own. Of *course*, we feel the full range of human emotions (*duh!?*) and get as frustrated or angry or judgmental as anybody else. It's simply that the way we communicate those feelings is specific to us, our upbringing, and our neighbors. Saying "I didn't really care for it" isn't a Midwestern *euphemism* for "The odiousness of what I just witnessed is all-consuming, and I will not rest until my leisure time is avenged"; it's just the way we say it! It isn't two-faced any more than "bonjour" is a two-faced way of communicating "hello."

At the same time, the Midwestern attitude toward others *is* something special. We *do* go out of our way for our neighbors and our guests. We *do* place a premium on making folks feel welcome and taken care of. We *do* have an extra cooler in the back of the Camry if ya need it for your trip to the lake; seriously, just let us know and we'll go right out and grab it for ya.

All this to say that this guide is about as far from laughing *at* the Midwest as you can get. It's laughing *with*, *for*, and *because of* the millions of wonderful people who make up the heart of this country—and the entirety of the Culver's rewards program. I want this guide to clarify your conversations. To start conversations. I want you and your friends to read a few pages out loud and then have to put the book down, next to the Tater-Tot casserole, while you share stories about which friend's finished basement was the best for playing truth-or-dare.

Whether you're looking to become a Midwesterner yourself, trying to communicate better with a middle-American loved one, preparing for a trip to the heartland (bring a jacket!), or just brushing up on your hometown lingo, I hope this book feels like a warm hug and a firm handshake (with eye contact).

This is *A Guide to Midwestern Conversation.*

Take off your coat and stay a while.

The Basics

Before we get into case-specific conversatin', it's important to review the most critical and universal tenets of the Midwestern language. From our "opes" to our "get outta heres," even the most generic of Midwestern expressions have very specific connotations.

Go 'head, dig on in!

"Ope! Lemme just squeeze right past ya."

Excuse me. I am already mid-squeeze but have gotten close enough that I need to acknowledge our proximity. I'll come and say goodbye to you before I leave.

"Jeez Louise."

Mother of God, what in the absolute hell? I am outraged, exhausted, and baffled all at once. I will now sigh and shake my head three times.

"Yeah, no."

No.

"No, yeah."

Yeah.

"You betcha!"

One hundred percent. Absolutely. I could not respond in a more affirmative manner.

"Mm-hmm. Yeah. You betcha."

I am finished with this conversation. I stopped listening some time ago. Let's wrap this up.

"Ope! Here I come, again!"

I need to get by you again, so I'm using our newfound familiarity to make it less awkward for both of us. If I see you in the parking lot, I'll wave enthusiastically.

"She's a doll."

I like her. She smiles a lot and agrees with everything I say.

"He's a real nice guy."

I like talking to him, and I've never seen him be rude or unkind to anyone. But our conversations have never been thorough enough for me to comment on anything but his general demeanor. I'll introduce you to him as "one of my favorite people."

"She/he is a character."

Absolutely out of her mind. Totally untethered by the norms of society. I go back and forth between finding her endearing and wanting to drop her off at a Hardee's in the middle of nowhere and never return. I'm spending one month's salary throwing her birthday party later this year.

"Nothin' gets past them."

Sharp as a tack, that one. Sometimes it's annoying, but we know they mean well.

"Does anybody wanna play cornhole?"

It is time for me to unleash the monster within. I will take down all of you with the fury of a tornado that absorbed another tornado and is now heading toward an open field. Sportsmanship has no place here. I am ready for war. For carnage. For the primitive hunger and undeniable arousal that comes from throwing beanbags accurately into the holes of a wooden ramp painted with the colors of my college or country. Who needs a beer before we start? I brought the YETI with me!

"Are you any good at cornhole?"

I'm here to effing win. Not interested in soothing your ego or "having a nice, chill time." I want blood. Will you join me? If you are actually bad, I will high-five you the whole time and encourage you with warmth and understanding.

"You're gettin' the hang of it."

You are not good at cornhole, but I am seeing improvement. If we win a game, I will call you the "clear MVP."

"That really tickled me."

I am beside myself with internal laughter. My world sparkles with your humor. I will tell the story of this moment at every dinner party, barbecue, and post-T-ball hangout until they put me in the ground. Every time I see you from this day forward, I will say, "Oh my gosh, remember when . . ." and then relive this amusing incident with you until I summon another person over and have you recount it for them. I will forevermore introduce you as "the funniest person I know."

"That's gonna be a bit of a challenge."

If I could scream "absolutely effing not!" in your face, I would. But I can't. I will, of course, exhaust every possible avenue to make your request happen.

"Let me get this one."

You may resist for four seconds, though it is futile. I said it first and therefore have staked my rightful claim to "this one." You can try to get the next one, but good luck with that. Seriously, good luck.

"Mm-hmmm, I hear ya"

For the love of God, shut up. I'm so bored. Like, sure, on a basic human level I understand your frustration. But I understood it the first thirty-seven times you said it. The next time I see you, my first question will be about this issue.

"I didn't really care for it."

What disaster hath humanity wrought? What hell has descended upon our fair planet that I must have, seared forever in my memory, that absolute monstrosity? I shudder to think that my descendants must come of age cohabitating with whatever the ever-loving hell that was. How could that incomprehensible scourge have come from the same planet that gave us cinnamon rolls, children's choirs, and calligraphy on distressed wood? My faith is shaken. I will claim to know the artist personally every time their name comes up from now on.

"Hey, question for ya!"

Something's been bugging me for the past week or so, and you're the most immediate authority that I know on the matter. I'll listen to your answer, and then go into a lot of detail about the thinking I've been doing over the past few days. From here on out, I'll text you every time this subject comes up.

"That could be fun!"

I mean exactly what I have just said. It *could* be fun. The *potential* is there. I need to think about how I feel without you looking at me. Do not get out your calendar, this is not a commitment of any kind. If I do decide to come, I will have the time of my life and thank you for this brilliant idea and diversion.

"Doesn't that sound fun?"

I don't care what you actually think. I want to do this, and I want you to agree to it with excitement right in this very moment so everyone can see. I will return the favor as soon as I'm able.

"Oh, now that's an idea!"

I had not considered that, and the fact that I had not considered that makes me think it is possibly a horrible idea. I will remain here, nodding to myself and staring into space, until I figure out my true feelings. To reenter the conversation, I will compliment you on whatever item of your clothing with which I am least familiar.

"You've really outdone yourself."

I am equal parts grateful, alarmed, and jealous. I don't think I've put this much energy into something since I sang Martina McBride's "Independence Day" at the school talent show when I was fourteen. I will make five more comments about this before we part ways.

"Well, I hope it works out for ya!"

I'm tired of talking about this now. Please stop before you go from grating to insufferable. I am genuinely invested in your success and will be asking for frequent updates.

"Well, there ya go."

Nothing more to be said. Nothing more to be done. Let's grab a beer.

"That's different!"

What in the ever-loving f*ck? Your [opinion/attire/home decor] is so actively displeasing to me that if someone offered me a lobotomy right now to forget about it, I would consider it. I am disgusted. I am confused. I have taken leave of my own body and ascended the astral plane just so I can make eye contact with my corporeal form and mouth, "*What is going on?*" I will explain it to the next person we see with genuine enthusiasm.

Midwestern Cursing

The Midwestern relationship with cursing is a complex, ever-evolving clusterf*ck. Some Midwesterners are proud to curse like sailors, while others take their distance from the ocean (and all naughty or nautical language) very seriously. Ever-industrious masters of language, however, we've found ways to get across the strong sentiments of swear words without "stooping to that level." (This book has also found a way around full-fledged cursing; it is called an asterisk.)

If you hear the following phrases over the course of your Midwestern chat, you are being cursed at. But not in a mean way! We swear!

"Oh, for crying out loud."
For f*ck's sake. Is this a f*cking joke?

"Get outta town."
Are you f*cking kidding me?

"Ya gotta help me out here."
Come the f*ck on.

"Well how 'bout that!"
That's f*cking great! Holy sh*t!!

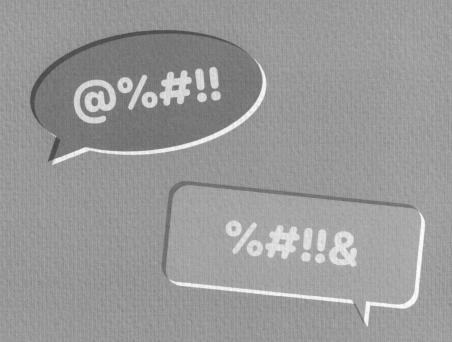

"Boy, I hear ya."
Shut the f*ck up.

"Excuse me?"
The f*ck did you just say?

"Dang it."
F*ck!

"Doggone it."
F*ck!

"Well, shoot."
F****cccckkkkk!

Illinois

NICKNAME: "Land of Lincoln"

REASON: Abraham Lincoln lived there!

He wasn't born there, and he didn't die there. But he was their senator, and he is buried there!

WHAT EVERYONE THINKS THE CAPITAL IS: Chicago

ACTUAL CAPITAL: Springfield

FAMOUS ILLINI

Betty White	Jennifer Hudson	Ray Croc
Bill Murray	Michelle Obama	Robin Williams
Ernest Hemingway (get real, Missouri)	Miles Davis	Ronald Reagan

PEOPLE WHO ARE FAMOUS BECAUSE OF WHAT THEY DID IN ILLINOIS

Mike Ditka	Tina Fey	The cow that knocked over the lantern that started the Great Chicago Fire
Scottie Pippen		

CLAIMS TO FAME

Chicago-Style Hot Dogs **Great Chicago Fire** **The Second City***

Deep-Dish Pizza **Lincoln's Log Cabin**

* Note: Chicago is not called The *Second* City because New York is the *first* city. Excuse you. It's because the Great Chicago Fire destroyed so much of the city that the one that stands now is considered Chicago 2.0!

LITTLE-KNOWN CLAIMS TO FAME

Garden of the Gods in Shawnee National Forest

Pumpkins
Illinois produces the most pumpkins in the country.

The Rockford Peaches
Along with the Blue Socks from South Bend, Indiana, the Rockford Peaches was one of only two teams to play all twelve years of the All-American Girls Professional Baseball League. The Peaches played from 1943 to 1954 and won championships in four of those years. Atta girls!

The World's Tallest Man
Robert Wadlow was born in Alton, Illinois. At his tallest, he measured 8 feet, 11 inches. Jeez Louise!.

World's largest ketchup bottle

IN-STATE CONFLICT

Chicago vs. The Rest of Illinois **Cubs vs. White Sox**

YOU CAN THANK ILLINOIS FOR

Cell phones **Pinball machines**

McDonald's **Zippers**

Arriving

The art of Midwestern Arrival Conversation is simple, but it requires ample preparation. Whether you're arriving to breakfast with a friend, coming into work for the day, or attending an event at another Midwesterner's home, you must be armed with the appropriate answers to the immediate questions about "the drive in" or "if it's still comin' down out there" and how every member of your family is doing, in intricate detail, preferably with pictures.

The Arrival also entails meeting any new people, firmly establishing the last time you saw one another, and offering to get anyone anything, no matter where you are or whether you are actually capable of getting them said thing.

From The Greeting to The Chit Chat to the exchanging of gifts, Midwestern Arrival Conversation is critical to establish conversation topics, gauge moods, and generally set the tone for the rest of your interaction: Super Friendly, Friendly, Tensely Friendly, or Angry Friendly.

When the Arrival takes place at someone's home (as opposed to an office or a coffee shop), guests and hosts alike also engage in the offering, accepting, or politely declining of first drinks. This is also the time for the customary "making excuses for" or "asking after" the people who have not yet made their own Arrival. It also coincides with the giving of the host/hostess gift, which we'll cover later in more detail, dontcha worry!

If you're nervous about your first Midwestern Arrival, or even just the next one coming up, remember that the Arrival is a team event. Everyone helps everyone get situated and get comfortable so you can get this show on the road!

Now . . . what can I getcha?

The Greeting

Kick off your conversation on the right foot. (Or the left if that works better! No worries either way!)

"Hey there, how's it going?"
I want to know how you are doing so that I can respond in an empathetic and appropriate way. Acceptable answers range from "good, thanks!" to "I just lost my uncle to prostate cancer and I'm unsure how to divide his estate with my mentally unstable brother." Either way, I want to hear about it and offer specific support and follow-up.

"Hi there."
I am either furious with you or in an incredible hurry. If we ever cross paths again, I will "apologize for being so short before" and give a detailed explanation for my behavior.

"Hey there, [name], good to meetcha."
We have never met before. Saying your name after you say it is a trick that I employ so I don't forget your name.

"Hey there, nice to see ya."
I want you to know that I know that we have met before, even if we don't have a super-strong relationship. In about five minutes, or at the next appropriate interval, I'll ask you to remind me where you live and offer specific compliments on the area.

"[Name], great to see you again."
You are important. I know you are important. I am saying your name so that you know that I know two things: your name, and that you are important.

"Well, they'll just let anybody into this place, won't they."
I like you so much! I like you so much! I like you so much! Seeing you is more exciting than getting a surprise onion ring on my cheeseburger or forgetting that it's Friday! I hope I am doing a good job of playing it cool

with my good-natured teasing. I recognize that you are otherwise occupied right now, so as soon as our interaction is over, I will say, "So great to see you, man," and then resist every urge in my body to invite you to hang out.

"Well, hey, stranger!"

I recognize that we haven't seen each other in a long time and feel the need to acknowledge it so you don't think that it's my desired state of affairs. Let's have the conversation that follows this greeting with a level of intimacy that matches our actual relationship rather than how little we've seen each other in the past year.

"Well, who do we have here?!"

I have noticed that you have a [child/dog/cat] and know that I should acknowledge it but do not know how you feel about me talking to it directly. Please guide me on how to proceed. I will no longer, for the rest of my life, be without a toy, gift, or smile for this person/animal.

"How was the drive in?"

These are the specifics that I'm looking for in your answer: Which route you took, how much traffic there was at what time in the morning, and whether you liked the view. I take great pride in my knowledge of the area and will offer detailed directions or modifications to your return trip.

"So sorry I'm late!"

I am ready to enumerate the multiple forces outside of my control that resulted in my tardiness. I will also apologize at the middle and end of our meeting as well as in my subsequent "it was so great to see you!" correspondence, whatever form that may take.

The Chit Chat

"Small Talk" is people making forced conversation out of social obligation. "Chit Chat" is Midwesterners making free-flowing, transitional conversation out of social obligation.

"I appreciate you making the time."

I understand that you are the person doing the favor in this scenario, and I want to be as respectful of your time as a pizza place with a thirty-minute delivery guarantee. Your thank-you gift basket is already in the mail.

"Mornin', everybody! How was the weekend?"

I want us to all go around the [table/break room/couch circle] and say how we spent our weekends. Who picked fruit? Who did nothing? Who went to that new place—that half of us will pretend to have heard about—and wants to tell us about how it's pretty cute but a little overpriced to be perfectly honest?

"Great setup ya got here."

I like your [office/TV room/kitchen] and am actively working to identify areas for decorative improvement so that I can send you a relevant gift. I'm thinking a woodcut of your favorite city's skyline.

"This is wonderful. I'm so glad we're getting the chance to do this."

I don't want you to mistake any lull in the conversation for disinterest or dissatisfaction. I've been excited about this for weeks, and sometimes that excitement might translate into reverent silence, like when you see a deer from the highway and just have to gaze at it for a second. I will text you ten minutes after we say goodbye to let you know how much fun I had.

Hosting

Making your home feel like everyone else's home while also anticipating their every need.

"You guys find the place okay?"

I sent you incredibly comprehensive directions in three different mediums, so the idea of you having trouble locating my very clearly marked home, covered in balloons, in the middle of the cul-de-sac, is inconceivable to me. If you had any issues, I would drive from my home to your home and draw an intricate map so that this doesn't happen again.

"Oh, you didn't need to bring anything!"

You were absolutely expected to bring something. If you hadn't, I would have asked if someone was sick or assumed you were raised by wild animals. When you leave, I will google the price of this item and bring something of equal or greater value the next time you host.

"Let me take your coats!"

We have designated the nearest bedroom as the coat closet for tonight. I will be throwing these on the bed as quickly as possible so I can get back to the party. At the end of the night, I will remember exactly which ones belong to whom.

"What can I getcha?"

Wine? Beer? Diet Coke? A cup of coffee that will require me to make a full pot even though no one else has asked for coffee or even intimated that it might be an option? All options are on the table. If your option isn't in the house or the garage fridge, I'll hop in my Sienna and head straight to Price Chopper.

"We're so sorry to miss [name], but maybe next time!"

Not sure what was so pressing that they had to miss an event for which we sent out a Paperless Post three weeks in advance, but whatever. I hope you interpret my lack of follow-up questions about their whereabouts for the bitterness and resentment it is. The next time that I see them, I will embrace them warmly, tell them how much we wish they'd been here, and reassure them that I completely understand.

— or —

When you told us you were coming alone, we almost spit out our local craft beer with joy. Their presence is usually the *steep* price we pay for enjoying your company. You are the ballpark hot dog; they are the extra four bucks we gotta pay if we want to eat and watch the game at the same time. The next time that we see you two together, we'll talk about how incomplete this event felt without them.

While this guide is, of course, intended to demystify the language of the landlocked, sometimes a phrase can mean different things depending on the context, person, or win/loss record of the local sports team. For these rare but real cases, this book will do its best to articulate all possible meanings. The final judgment, though, rests with you.

"Shoes by the door, if you please!"

Honestly, I can't believe it isn't your first instinct to take off your disgusting shoes before entering someone else's home. Do you believe yourself immune to the dirt and grime of the outside world? I will now effusively compliment your shoes even if—especially *if*—I have seen them before.

Your First Arrival

Midwesterners pride themselves on being able to remember small, meaningful things about each new person they meet. More often than not, that thing will be *the most memorable or strange thing* you do, say, or claim during this introductory period. Proceed with caution. Sure, the new fountain pen you got at a thrift shop might be burning a hole in your conversational pocket, but unless you want to get a pen for every birthday or be inundated with thrift-shop recommendations for the rest of your interactions with these people, keep it to yourself during that first meeting. Also, most personal facts you share will get what's called the Midwestern Telephone Treatment: they'll be increasingly embellished in your favor as they spread from person to person.

Example

"I live in Massachusetts, and I am a science teacher."

Will eventually become

"Oh, she/he is a super-smartie. A professor at MIT or something!"

Attending

Be a gracious and appreciative guest while also trying to have as few needs as possible to take the pressure off the host/hostess.

"This a shoes-off house?"

Does this family think they can somehow defend their precious homestead from the unchecked chaos that is the elements of the outdoors? You'd really prefer that I explore your home in stockings or the bottom-most skin of my body because you think that's *less gross*? My eyes haven't rolled this far back in my head since they tried to "modernize" the local dive bar. The next time that we come over, we will get family pedicures in advance.

"My sister's husband also has a shoes-off rule!"

I hate my sister's husband.

"We just broughtcha a little something."

Twenty-five minutes before we left the house, I remembered that we needed a hostess gift. Everything you see here, from the bag to the cute little ribbon, has been in my gift closet for longer than I can remember. If you don't like it, I will surreptitiously leave the party and come back with an expensive ($25) bottle of wine.

"[Mutual friend who I'm slightly closer to than you] is on their way!"

Yeah, that's right. We're texting about your event and they're giving *me* updates instead of you. I just want you to remember that even though *you're* hosting the gathering, I still possess a lot of social capital. We've been discussing my impression of this event already, and we *will* debrief between ourselves on our ways home. Before we leave, we'll both invite you to grab drinks with us next week.

"I'm okay for now."

I want a beverage badly, but I wasn't immediately prepared with an answer, and it doesn't look like everyone else is drinking yet, so I will wait until it's more socially acceptable to request one or sneak off and acquire one on my own. If I end up a de facto bartender bringing drinks to everyone over the course of this event, so be it!

"Sure, I'll take a [beverage]."

I'm too thirsty to demure! When I return later for a refill, I'll bring one of whatever you're having as well.

Host/Hostess Gifts

It may be the thought that counts, but it's the gift that says "I only remembered thirty-five minutes ago that this was happening."

Cute Hand Towels That Match the Home Decor

WHAT THE GIFT SAYS: "I loved these when I bought them. They don't go with the colors in my guest bathroom, but I need them to exist out in the world so I put them on the gift shelf. I grabbed them when I realized that I forgot to chill the wine I was going to bring."

WHAT YOU SAY WHILE GIVING THE GIFT: "How cute are those, right? I saw them in HomeGoods weeks ago and I thought, '[host's name] HAS to have these,' so when I got your invite I was, like, today's the day! You can return them, I have a gift receipt."

A Bottle of White Wine (Chilled)

WHAT THE GIFT SAYS: "This is the wine that I want to drink, if I had the option, so feel free to open it now. It was either already in my fridge for me to drink and I grabbed it on my way out the door, *or* I just bought it on the way over."

WHAT YOU SAY WHILE GIVING THE GIFT: "Just brought you a little something in case you didn't have enough, hahaha! Just kidding! This one is *for you*, no sharing. It is my favorite, though, so do let me know what you think! Thank you again for having us. Gosh, your house is gorgeous!"

A Bottle of White Wine (Warm)

WHAT THE GIFT SAYS: "This is a random bottle of wine from my gift closet that I did not chill. I either trust our friendship enough to know that you won't care that it's not ready to serve, or I think so little of our relationship that I don't care if you think it's rude."

WHAT YOU SAY WHILE GIVING THE GIFT: "Here you go! Sorry it's not chilled. I bought it two weeks ago as soon as you invited us because it's one of my favorites and, honestly, you have to try it! It's actually better that you can't serve it right now, because I want it to be all for you. No sharing! Okay, how can I help? Put me to work!"

A Bottle of Red Wine

WHAT THE GIFT SAYS: "You'll never know if I bought this today or if it was a secret Santa gift from my office in 2014. You'll never know if I care enough about this event to remember to chill the wine. I have vanquished you in the tête-à-tête of hostess gifts. Your move. Yes, I say . . . *your* move."

WHAT YOU SAY WHILE GIVING THE GIFT: "Thank you so much for having us! We brought a little somethin' somethin'! What are you drinking? I'll grab you another on my way back."

A Bouquet of Flowers

WHAT THE GIFT SAYS: "There are no liquor stores on the drive to your home, but there is a florist."

WHAT YOU SAY WHILE GIVING THE GIFT: "I figured a lot of people were bringing wine, and I thought I could do something a little more personal. They're lovely, right? No, *no*, don't you move—I'll put them in water myself!"

Coasters

WHAT THE GIFT SAYS: "These offer me an opportunity to tell a story about a trip I took or an artist I know, and you bet your ass I'm gonna do it right now."

WHAT YOU SAY WHILE GIVING THE GIFT: "Okay, now I gotta tell you about these. These are from Bogotá, Colombia, where my son-in-law was born. They're made by this amazing group that contracts local women, pays them a living wage, and lets them create their own designs! How amazing, right? I thought, I *have* to get these for all my friends. And now you can tell the story! My bag is from Colombia too! Do you want it? I have another one at home! Everything is so cheap there!"

A Candle

WHAT THE GIFT SAYS: "I bought fifteen of these at the HomeGoods after-Christmas sale."

WHAT YOU SAY WHILE GIVING THE GIFT: "It's just a little something to say thanks for having us. We have one in our house, too, and we love it, it just smells *great*."

This Book

WHAT THE GIFT SAYS: "I love you and deeply value you as a friend. I care so fiercely about your happiness that I have spent a full $16.99 to give you the exquisite and joyful gift of self-referential humor and inside-the-coasts jokes. I also find the author very beautiful!"

WHAT YOU SAY WHILE GIVING THE GIFT: "This book is just *so fun*. I flipped through a few pages in the store, and I just could not stop laughing. I also find the author very beautiful!"

Indiana

NICKNAME: "The Hoosier State"

REASON

It's debated by scholars and Hoosiers alike! Some say it's because surveyors who came upon Indiana while it was first being settled by English speakers would call out "Who's Here?"—later shortened to "Hoosiers." Others claim the nickname derived from a man named Samuel Hoosier, who used to say he preferred to hire laborers from Indiana. But no record of a man with that name exists, so honestly, who knows!

WHAT EVERYONE THINKS THE CAPITAL IS: Indianapolis

ACTUAL CAPITAL: Indianapolis

FAMOUS HOOSIERS

Brendan Fraser	James Dean	Michael Jackson
Cole Porter	John Wooden	Skylar Diggins-Smith
Harold Hill	Larry Bird	

FAMOUS PEOPLE WHO SPENT TIME IN INDIANA, SO IT COUNTS

Abraham Lincoln	Mark Spitz
Adam Driver	Sasheer Zamata

Hoosiers (basketbal team)	*Hoosiers* (movie)	Indianapolis 500

LITTLE-KNOWN CLAIMS TO FAME

The Most Midwestern Manhunt Ever

In 1972, a man named Martin McNally skyjacked an airplane and collected more than $500,000 in ransom before parachuting out over Peru, Indiana. He accidentally dropped the money on his way down and it landed in a bean field where it was spotted by Lowell Elliott (the field belonged to his son-in-law). McNally fell into a field a few miles away, got a ride into town from the police chief, and then stayed in a hotel there for three nights. Elliott, meanwhile, returned the money and, despite being offered $10,000 and an all-expenses trip from American Airlines, said he didn't like flying and would rather have a cool $25,000 instead. American Airlines said no. Lowell Elliott ended up with nothing. It is the wildest story ever told.

Santa Claus

Every year, volunteer "elves" from Santa Claus, Indiana, send personalized replies to the thousands of children's letters mailed to Santa in care of the local post office.

YOU CAN THANK INDIANA FOR

Chuck Taylor sneakers (aka Converse All Stars)	"Take Me Out to the Ballgame" (melody)	Theme parks
Seat belts		

Dining

Many Midwestern conversations take place over food, about food, or while buying food in order to make a different kind of food (probably casserole!). Eating together in our landlocked locales involves not only meeting the dietary needs of yourself, guests, and family, but also commenting on your dishes with the appropriate mix of information and praise.

When dining out with loved ones or liked ones, picking a place to eat is a delicate dance of light suggestions, playful hints, and actively figuring out what sounds good to you. The trick with Midwestern meal companions is that we're less sure about where we want to eat than we are about where we do not want to eat. Mastering this process of elimination takes years to perfect. Novices can get around it by suggesting a location *within* the dining invitation: "Do you want to grab lunch at Houlihan's tomorrow? I've been craving their Caesar."

Once at the chosen/unobjected-to restaurant, Midwesterners engage in table chatter, both among themselves and with the server. Topics include weather, sports, how business is going, or a story about the last time they ate here. The conversational aspect of the meal might temporarily supersede the "deciding," "ordering," and "eating" part, so you might want to have a few snacks on the drive there, just in case.

Servers in the heartland also have a language all their own, an intricate spoken code that transforms "you eat like a pack of rabid raccoons" into a sweet "can I get those outta the way for ya?"

Finally, there is the at-home dinner party where hosts and guests alike must compliment, assist with, serve, and gauge the quality of the meal while the chef is in the room. Whether we're put "in charge of dessert" or firmly instructed to "grab a glass of wine and a seat!" any Midwesterner worth their table salt must master the art of talking with their mouth full of compliments.

Choosing a Place

Making your preferences known—but not too much.

"What are we all in the mood for?"

I don't want to be the one who makes this decision, so I'm throwing this one to the group and praying with everything inside me that someone makes a definitive statement within the next thirty seconds. If no one does, I will ask follow-up questions that demand consensus until someone requests a place. If no one does, I will suggest the new restaurant in town or the place we ate last time, in that order.

"I could really go for some . . ."

I desperately want this and have been thinking about it all day. If someone objects, I will gladly defer to their wants.

"I wouldn't say no to some . . ."

Ooooh, you know, that does sound good. I hadn't thought about it until right now, but now the prospect of it consumes me. I will thank whoever suggested this option for their great idea three times over the course of the meal.

"We actually had that for lunch."

Nope. Next option. Unless you're really craving it, then okay.

"I'd actually prefer somewhere else if that's all right."

That suggestion fills me with disgust. I had to actively stop myself from retching when you brought it up, and I must now rethink all of my impressions about your taste. I would rather teach a squirrel to square dance than eat one morsel from that hellhole. I'll get you a gift certificate from that restaurant as soon as I can.

As a Diner

Getting your menu questions answered, offering comments on the food, and asking for a few more minutes every few minutes.

"Could I bother you for some . . ."

In any intelligent universe, this thing would have come out with my order. But I guess I'll flag you down since you're going to make me beg like a child who just heard the ice-cream truck. When you come back in ten minutes, empty-handed, I will apologize for being so difficult.

"Sorry! We just need a few more minutes, thanks!"

We were talking and forgot we were in a restaurant. We need, conservatively, another half hour to even think about food. You will need to come back a minimum of two more times. Thank you, Kayley. (Of course, we remember your name!)

"We hated it."

As you can tell by my immaculately clean plate, this dish more than met my standards for a good, hearty meal. I will now take your pleasant laughter as a sign of a job well done rather than an exhausted attempt at appeasing the maker of a joke you've heard four times tonight.

"The [specific dish] here is great."

I assume full responsibility for your dining experience if you take my recommendation. I shall spend the time between your order and the delivery of the food in a state of suspended anticipation, excitement, and dread. If you seem anything less than transcendently happy with your meal, I will personally order you something different.

"It's not my favorite."

If they serve food in hell, this is it. As bland as a car bumper without stickers and as overwhelming as the variety of items in the Cracker Barrel Old Country Store. But not in a good way. I will eat at least half the food on my plate so our server doesn't notice.

"I'd have some if ya ordered it."

I want to eat it, but I do not want to be responsible for suggesting it. Your willingness to make the request will not go unnoticed or unrewarded.

— or —

I will subtly but definitely fight you for each morsel as soon as it hits the table. The last bite will remain on the plate until you give in to my demands that you take it.

"Ooh, that looks good!"

Hello, stranger! That thing you have on your plate looks like something I might want to eat! Please tell me what it is and if you like it. If you're still here when I leave, I will high-five you and tell you how wonderful it was.

"Now tell me a little more 'bout what's in that."

I kind of want to be adventurous in my eating but I am terrified of change or risk. Please enumerate every single ingredient in the dish so that I am not surprised when it comes out or so that, if I chicken out, I can blame one of those ingredients rather than my inability to try new things. If I do end up ordering it, I will tell you it's the best thing I've ever tasted no matter what.

"My doctor's on me about my cholesterol."

My blood is mostly beer and beer batter with some red meat and potatoes mixed in. I don't actually believe that subbing a side salad for onion rings will fix that problem, but it certainly makes me feel better!

"Could ya do that without the _____ ?"

I could pick this ingredient out of the dish myself but I do not want to. If you cannot, I will probably just order the burger.

"What's your favorite?"

I'm not craving anything in particular, and my day has left me unprepared to be responsible for this decision. If I don't like any of the things you suggest, I'll probably just order the burger.

As the Server

Going over the specials, laughing at bad jokes, and pretending like you're not doing it all for the tips.

"Before we get started, I do want to let you know what we're out of . . ."

Please don't be mad. Please don't be mad. Please don't be mad. I forgot to do this list for my last table and then they ordered three things we were out of (potato skins, Southwestern spring rolls, and queso) and tipped me $5 on $80. I had to go cry in the walk-in for five minutes. If you don't look disappointed by anything I list, I will bring you a free appetizer.

"Can I start you off with some mozzarella sticks or spin dip?"

Would you like to add 75 cents to my tip?

"What are we drinkin' tonight? Bucket of beer? Pitcher of watermelon margaritas? Bottle of wine?"

Would you like to add $2 to my tip?

"Would you all like to hear the specials?"

Would you like to add $1.50 to my tip and help me win the competition between servers for who sells the most specials tonight? The prize is a gift card to Menards.

"Is Pepsi okay?"

I know it is but I have to ask, because the one time I didn't ask, a guy flipped out and then my manager cut my hours and I was fifty bucks short on the kids-size electric Volkswagen Beetle that I was going to buy for my niece's birthday (so she could win "slug bug" every time she went into the garage!). If you really want Coke, I'd be happy to grab you one from the trunk of my Sonata.

"I'm not sure if we can do that, but I can go ask the chef for ya."

You miserable, high-maintenance scourge. Your weird dietary preferences just made my night more difficult than explaining Sonic Drive-In to a European. Oh well, time to shuffle back to the kitchen and let the chef berate me because you think all of life is as customizable as a Chipotle bowl. When I drop off your check I will write, "Thanks so much!" and draw a little smiley face.

"How is everything tasting?"

I hope everything that I recommended to you tastes good and secretly hope you're slightly dissatisfied with any decisions you made against my advice. If anything is not exactly how you like it, I will fix it and bring you free dessert.

"Looks like you hated it!"

I see you have wiped your plate clean like a high school band at a carwash in the Hy-Vee parking lot. Hopefully, this jovial reminder that you thoroughly enjoyed your meal will propel your generosity through dessert all the way to the tip portion of the receipt. I'll recommend this dish to the next table I serve.

"Did we save room for dessert?"

Looks like your meal's over, which means it's time for you to either order more food so I can make more money or leave so I can seat another table and make more money. Either way, we'll have a pleasant conversation about our local sports team for five minutes.

"Thank you for your patience."

This is one of the top-five worst days of my entire existence, and I am surrounded by incompetent Neanderthals who move at the speed of an 18-wheeler at rush hour. But you did not make it worse. And for that, I am eternally in your debt. Please accept these drinks that I ordered from the bartender as an excuse to go to the bar for a shot of whiskey to get me through the rest of the night.

Midwestern Menu

APPETIZERS

Dip with a Cheese Base

Dip with a Vaguely Vegetable Cheese Base

Deep-Fried Spring Roll

[Region-Specific] Fried Cheese

Chicken Tenders (Buffalo Tenders if it's a fancy place)

Nachos

Popcorn Shrimp

"Loaded" [Region-Specific Potato Item]

SOUPS AND SALADS

Soup of the Day

One Other Soup (probably cheese-based)

Caesar Salad
(add chicken $3, salmon $4, or blackened shrimp $13)

House Salad
(bacon, eggs, tortilla chips, creamy dressing,
possibly sprinkled with lettuce)

SANDWICHES AND WRAPS
Served with fries or a salad*

Club Sandwich

Burger

The Same Burger but with Bacon (costs $3 more)

BLT That Also Contains Another Type of Protein

Caesar Salad Wrap

Buffalo Chicken Wrap

Grilled Chicken Breast on Ciabatta Bread
with Two Other Semi-High-End Ingredients (costs $17)

* Warm mixed greens, three pieces of tomato, raw red onion,
diced cucumber, and your choice of dressing packet!

[*Inexplicable*]

HOUSE SPECIALTIES

Fajitas

Chicken Alfredo

Salmon

Steak (market price)

Chicken Pot Pie

Flatbread That Is Actually Just a Square Pizza

SIDES

French Fries

Alternative Fried Potato Side That Is $1 More Expensive
(your choice of sweet potato fries or Tater Tots)

Baked Potato

Mixed Vegetables That Were Gonna Go Bad
If They Weren't Cooked Today (ask your server)

Mac 'n' Cheese

Green Beans with Little Bits of Ham

KIDS MENU

Chicken Nuggets

Mac 'n' Cheese That Is Somehow Not the Same as the Mac 'n' Cheese Side

Hot Dog

DESSERTS

Molten Lava Cake

Obscenely Large Baked-Good Sundae (brownie or cookie)

"New York–Style" Cheesecake from the Nearest Grocery Store

Scoops of Ice Cream

Dining at Someone's Home

Selecting, eating, and complimenting food all in the presence of the chef who is also your friend. No pressure!

"Dinner's at Six!"

We will be sitting down to eat at 6 p.m. I know you will probably get here forty–five minutes early and I have prepared for that eventuality by putting out a few snacks. I also started panic cleaning at three o'clock instead of four.

"What can I help you with?"

I am absolutely starving, and it looks like we'll be eating a little bit later than I anticipated, so I am willing to do *anything* to speed this process along. This also provides me with an excuse to steal bites of appetizers under the guise of "giving something a try." When we actually do sit down, I'll loudly announce that you did everything.

"Put me to work!"

I like you more than anyone else who is here so far, so I'd rather stay in the kitchen and keep busy than have to chit chat. I plan to compliment literally everything you do as you do it.

"What's already open? I don't want you to open a new bottle for me."

Wine is wine. Whatever you already have is gonna get the job done. When we kill that one, we can open the one I brought.

— or —

I specifically want the rosé I saw in the fridge when I was helping you grab the shrimp cocktail sauce, but I would rather eat a cinnamon roll without icing than say that out loud. If we do end up opening that bottle, I will serve everyone before myself.

"What's wrong? You not hungry?"

If I get a hint that you're not eating for any other reason than your body does not feel like it requires food, I will get in my Chevy Impala and scour the three supermarkets in our area (even the expensive one where we only go for special occasions) to find something that you will enjoy eating. I will glance warmly over at you to check your status every three to four minutes.

Iowa

NICKNAME: "The Hawkeye State"

REASON: Many say it was a tribute to a Sauk tribe leader named Black Hawk.

Black Hawk was forced off his native land and into Iowa. No one can smooth things over and pretend they're better like Midwesterners, that's for sure.

WHAT EVERYONE THINKS THE CAPITAL IS: Des Moines

ACTUAL CAPITAL: Des Moines

FAMOUS IOWANS

Ashton Kutcher	Donna Reed	Johnny Carson
"Buffalo Bill" Cody	Grant Wood	N.K. Jemisin
Cloris Leachman	John Wayne	

FAMOUS PEOPLE WHO SPENT TIME IN IOWA, SO IT COUNTS

Harold Hill	Jason Momoa

Bridges of Madison County

Corn

That's right. Of all the states in all the Midwest, Iowa produces the most of our country crop. Would it be too corny to put a joke here? Yeah . . . probably.

Iowa Writers' Workshop

The University of Iowa hosts the oldest writers workshop in the nation. It's also one of the most prestigious. Wordsmiths such as Raymond Carver, Yaa Gyasi, Rita Dove, Flannery O'Connor, and Carmen Maria Machado all spent a little time pushing the pen in Iowa City. In fact, Iowa City is the only UNESCO City of Literature in the United States! Get outta town!

LITTLE-KNOWN CLAIMS TO FAME

Gymnastic champion training ground!

Two All-Around Gold Medalists: Shawn Johnson and Gabby Douglas

An island town

That's right, Sabula, Iowa (population 506), sits between two lakes and is technically an island city! The whole thing is one mile long and one-quarter mile wide, and while it's not exactly a surfing spot, the hiking, boating, fishing, and camping are about as unique as it gets in the Midwest

YOU CAN THANK IOWA FOR

Butterfly stroke   **Red Delicious apples**   **Sliced bread**

Those kids have a lot of energy

4

Parenting

Midwestern parenting is a delicate dance of love and self-restraint. Like all parents, Midwestern moms and dads juggle their kiddos' social lives, health care, academic success, and general existence in the world all while trying to be full, happy humans themselves. They find refuge in other parents who understand that a kid having "a lot of energy" is a cry for help, while a warning that someone might be "a little shy" means they can expect total silence while hiding behind mom's skirt for the duration of the interaction.

When talking with their kids, Midwesterners employ a balance of helpful, direct advice and thinly veiled exasperation. Midwestern kids know to be just as nervous about the words "have a seat," as they are about the use of their full names. And while Midwestern parents certainly have plenty of different ways of saying "no," they also have their own special ways to say "yes."

Conversing with and about other parents requires honesty with more than a hint of finesse. Midwesterners have a way of speaking that is designed to give true reviews of other people's children and their own. Judging someone else's parenting choices is rude, and a Midwesterner would never dare. Instead, we summarize what we believe to be their parenting philosophy ("easygoing," "a tight ship," "sports-focused") and let the comment hang suspended in the air like water in July.

Then, of course, there is parenting in front of other parents: talking to our kiddos in the presence of other adults. In the Midwest, two conversations happen concurrently. One is, "This is information that I want to impart to you, my child." The other is, "This is how I parent. This is how calm and collected I am all the time."

Regardless of how Midwestern parents feel at any given moment, the prevailing sentiment of parenting here is always love. Love for our young ones. Love for the community helping us raise them. And love for the wonderful Midwestern adults they will one day become.

Conversations with Your Kids

Making yourself clear while staving off tantrums.

"Ask your mother."
> The last time I gave you permission to do something, your mother got very upset with me and we didn't speak on the entire date-night drive to Golden Corral. I couldn't even enjoy the unlimited Jumbo Butterfly Shrimp.

"Ask your father."
> The last time I gave you permission to do something, your father got very upset with me and we didn't speak on the entire date-night drive to Culver's. I couldn't even enjoy my ButterBurger.

"You may want to rethink that."
> I am giving you one more chance, at the height of my patience, to get your act together before our afternoon trip to the water park turns into you scrubbing your entire bathroom with the brush we use to get ice off the Suburban. If you show appropriate remorse, we will stop for ice cream on the way.

"So if I call _____ 's mom, she'll tell me the same thing?"
> The jig is absolutely up.

"Maybe."
> No.

"We'll see."
> No.

"Is your room clean?"
> Ha ha. No.

"I don't have a problem with that."
> Yes.

"It's all right with me."

Yes. But I want to acknowledge that I might not be the only person with "permission granting" power in this scenario, and I want to extend the other person the same veto privilege that I would expect them to offer me were the roles reversed. If it doesn't work out, I will let you choose what you want for dinner out of sympathy.

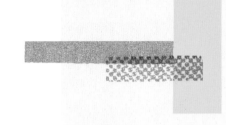

"We'll figure something out."

Yes. It might be complicated, but I want this to happen for you as much as you do.

"What'd you do at school today?" (to a child in elementary school)

Please go into completely adorable but incoherent detail about your day while I drive home as fast as I can before you realize that I have forgotten your snack and you have a total breakdown.

"What'd you do at school today?" (to a teen)

Please share *something*. Any shred of insight into your life, interests, or relationships. If you say "not much," I will die a little inside and then take you to Starbucks.

"Have a seat. We're gonna have a chat."

You are in for it. Your life will now be divided into the world you knew before this moment and the world you know after it. Whatever you think might be about to happen, the reality is ten times worse. Cancel whatever plans you had until you graduate.

Conversations with Your Kids in Front of Other Parents

Showing the whole world what a levelheaded, patient parent you can pretend to be.

"Do you want to show [name] your toy/dance move/etc.?"

Ha! It's your turn now, sucker. Get ready for a glimpse, one small peek into what my daily life is like with these attention-hungry youth thieves. If you don't "awww!" and "wow!" and "well look at that!" as though your life depended on it, I'm going to invite you to their next living-room performance of *Daniel Tiger: The Musical*. The seats are on the floor and the popcorn is somehow always wet. Obviously, our next happy hour is on me.

"What do we say when someone gives us a present?"

Dammit, child. We have been working on manners all freakin' month for literally *this* occasion and you go and let me down like this? *Come on.* When you're a teenager, I swear to God, I am going to embarrass you with the frenzy, fervor, and confidence of a Girl Scout selling cookies at the office where her mom is CEO.

"We're going to go inside and have some quiet time."

I'm going inside and will scream into a pillow while binge-eating my children's Halloween candy.

"Whatever happened to that [last name] kid?"

My experience with this child is seared into my brain. I was so taken with their personality and general antics that I think of them every time I am around other kids my child's age. I also have an excellent story to share about them, but you can go first.

Conversations with Other Parents

Walking the fine line between commiserating, gossiping, complaining, and accidentally offering to babysit for free.

"[Our kid] has been having some issues."

Help me. *Please*. Send therapists, send sedatives, send that lady at the church who is some kind of mean but who all the kids apparently love. My life is noisier than a first Wednesday in tornado season, and even taking an hour to myself every day to walk around JOANN's isn't helping. But enough about me, what brings *you* to this garage sale?

"We're working on using our inside voices."

The screaming. Please, someone stop the screaming. The decibel level in my house reaches "opposing team shooting a free-throw at a college basketball game" at least twice an hour. Sometimes I just sit in my Highlander in the TJ Maxx parking lot to absorb the momentary quiet. I have a secret calendar under my bed counting down the number of days before it will be socially acceptable to leave them at home by themselves.

"They're pretty easygoing parents."

Their lives are unbridled chaos, and their children are free from the bonds of any discipline whatsoever. Once, I saw the younger one trying to eat a freeze pop in the park with his (shoeless!) feet. I am at once appalled by their tranquility while envious of their seeming infallibility in the face of anarchy. We've invited them to stay at our lake house.

"They run a pretty tight ship over there."

Jeez Louise, let the kids *breathe*! That house has got more rules than a Holiday Inn swimming pool. They're just absolutely asking for an all-out rebellion before the age of twenty. Swear to God, those kids' first words were, "I'm not allowed to." We're having them over for dinner next week.

"Does _____ want to come over for a playdate?"

Let us enter into the age-old bargain of child transfer. Today, the young one that you've sired will take shelter under my roof, eat of my Chef Boyardee, and play in my train-themed playroom. You shall, in their absence, perform whatever rituals you require, whether they be "spending one-on-one time with the baby," "stopping by the Price Chopper to get flour tortillas," or "just sitting down for one goddamn minute." On the morrow, or another day of your choosing, you shall return the favor, removing my spawn from my home, so that I, too, may "run some errands" or "watch a show where two consenting adults get it on." I will send your offspring home with some baked goods for you.

"Our kids are friends."

I don't want you thinking that I interact with that person of my own accord. I will send their family a custom Christmas card and bake them Pillsbury Shape cookies for the holiday season.

"Those kids have a lot of energy."

Monsters. They are *monsters*. I have never once requested compensation for babysitting them.

"I love all my children equally."

Cumulatively, that's probably accurate. But today, I love the one who didn't get caught skipping practice to make out in the parking lot a *little* bit more. And yesterday, I loved the one who thought it would be fun to microwave the entire metal pot of Annie's mac and cheese a *little* less.

"We'd love to, but it's just a bit tough with the kids."

We could make the effort if we really wanted to, but we don't. So, we are employing the oldest, most sacred tradition of blaming our offspring. I love those little ready-made excuses more than anything. I will ask repeatedly about this event the next time I see you and echo my regret.

"Keep an eye on that one."

This is an endearing monster child. Not all monster children are endearing, but this one is. When they graduate in ten years, I'll get them an extra-special present.

"Are kids invited?"

Is this a "family fun" situation or a "hire a babysitter and get a little drunk" situation? Either way, I will come bearing on-theme gifts and refreshments.

"Bring the kids!"

We want to see you! We miss you! Where are you? Are you okay? Are you drowning in diapers and soccer practice? This is part friend outing and part vitality check. It will be like a Pixar movie: a kid-friendly, adult experience. I will hand each of your children a five-dollar bill on sight.

"It's nice to have a kid-free night every once in a while."

This is amazing. Why did we even have children? I miss them already. When can we go home?

A GUIDE TO
"Appropriate for Kids"

"Is it appropriate for kids?" is a *trick question* in the Midwest. Do not take the bait—no matter how many times you and the one asking have agreed about the state of your local sports team! No two people have the same threshold for child appropriateness. One person's "totally fine" is another person's "You said the word *stupid* and my child is scarred for life—we will never compliment your pinwheels again." The best way to navigate this question is to relate the facts so that the responsibility is on another person or ratings organization.

Example

YOU: Hi, Mr. Cullingsworth, we'd love for Henrietta to come over for a playdate today and watch the new film *An Animated Pony Faces Adversity but Then Learns an Important Developmental Lesson.*

MR. CULLINGSWORTH: Is it appropriate for kids?

YOU: It is rated G by the Motion Picture Association of America, a designation that means "for all ages."

Then, if little Henrietta can't handle the cold, hard truth that "we can all be winners if we work as a team!" that's not on you. That's on the MPAA.

Conversations with the Babysitter

Trying to have a nice dinner without asking for a kids menu.

"Help yourself to whatever's in the fridge."
I really mean that. I will check to see what you eat large amounts of so I can stock more for your next visit. If that sounds like a bribe, it is. We need you to come back. Please don't leave us.

"Call us if there's an emergency."
I am putting all my faith and the quality of my evening in my belief that you understand the difference between an emergency and a whiny child.

"Did the kids behave okay?"
I only want to know if someone got maimed or learned a new curse word. Otherwise, just say yes.

Kansas

NICKNAME: "The Sunflower State"

REASON: It's the fourth-largest producer of sunflowers in the United States.

(Yes, the other three are in the Midwest but that would be so *rude* to point out.)

WHAT EVERYONE THINKS THE CAPITAL IS: Wichita

ACTUAL CAPITAL: Topeka

FAMOUS KANSANS

Amelia Earhart	Dorothy Gale	Janelle Monáe
Buster Keaton	Gwendolyn Brooks	Melissa Etheridge
	Hattie McDaniel	

FAMOUS PEOPLE WHO WERE BORN IN KANSAS CITY, KANSAS (KANSAS CITY, MISSOURI, CAN SUCK IT)

Charlie Parker

FAMOUS PEOPLE WHO SPENT TIME IN KANSAS, SO IT COUNTS

Clark Kent/Superman

Dwight D. Eisenhower

James Naismith

Jason Sudeikis

John Brown

Langston Hughes

Paul Rudd

William S. Burroughs

CLAIMS TO FAME

Heart of the Heartland

Actually, heart of the *whole* land. Smith County, Kansas, is the geographical center of the contiguous United States!

Kansas is *literally* flat as a pancake. Seriously, they did a topographical comparison.

LITTLE-KNOWN CLAIMS TO FAME

The *actual* windiest city in the United States is Dodge City, Kansas.

The Cosmosphere

Well, how 'bout that! You can go to space camp in the middle of Kansas. What started out as a planetarium now holds the largest combined collection of Russian and US space artifacts in the world. (The Russians have more Russian artifacts, and the Smithsonian has more US stuff.)

IN-STATE CONFLICT

K-State vs. KU

YOU CAN THANK KANSAS FOR

Basketball

Sure, technically the game was "first played" in Massachusetts, but that state absolutely lost its privileges.

The ICEE

5

That kid is special

8086 ✳

Sports

Sports conversation in the Midwest starts early and doesn't end until we're six feet under, buried in our favorite jersey. Youth games take over weekends as early as first grade, and the Big Decision is: Do you want to converse with the parent who thinks "it's really nice that they don't keep score at this age" or with the parent who's tallying up points on a notepad in between sips of their Big Gulp coffee because "competition isn't a four-letter word, you know." If you are a child, of course, just have fun playing and do not sit by any of the parents. They will give you plenty of advice about your game when you get to high school.

Beyond their high school rivalries, Midwestern cities have two sets of sports allegiances: college and professional. Picking a college team can be as simple as a die-hard, almost pathological devotion to your alma mater or as intricate as deciding to favor the rival of your parents' school just to keep things interesting while you shovel mom's famous spin dip into your mouth.

Some cities have their own professional sports team. The spoiled Midwestern ones have two teams in the same major-league sport (looking at you, Chicago). Professional sports allegiances are fickle, fraught relationships that bring the highest of highs and the lowest of lows—and that's not just because it's dadgum near impossible nowadays to find the games on TV.

Regardless of your alliance, the Midwest sports world is an equal opportunity trash-talk community. Somewhere in our heads we know that wrapping our emotional well-being in the athleticism of strangers isn't the healthiest thing. But like turning down a third round of twenty-five-cent wings—there are some things ya just gotta do for your heart.

Youth Sports

Consistently reminding yourself and everyone around you that they're just kids and it's just a game.

"That kid is special, huh?"

My adulation and adoration are all-consuming. I know more about the eating and sleeping habits of this fifteen-year-old phenom than I know about my own cardiac health. My infatuation exhilarates me, but it also scares me, like all the sauce options at Buffalo Wild Wings. If I ever saw the kid in public, I would nod politely and move on.

"Well, she's just a good little player."

If it were in any way appropriate for me to kneel at the altar of a thirteen-year-old, I would. Her skills fill me with a combination of unmatched pride and white-hot jealous rage at my own deficiencies. I would buy her Red Robin hamburgers for the rest of my life if it meant she would never age, graduate, or otherwise deprive me of witnessing her incredible athletic talent. When I see her in the grocery store this weekend, I will say "Great game" and nothing else.

"He's just not as far along."

If that pathetic excuse for an athlete were my child, I would never show my face in public again. Each mistake he makes is more excruciating than the last, and it challenges my faith in God to be presented with such profound mediocrity. I can't wait to talk to his parents after this and tell them how much he's improved and how proud I am.

"We'll get 'em next time."

I wish I could ask for a refund for that game. Not in money, in minutes of life. I could have spent that time fixing my Jeep or hanging the Christmas lights or googling why Mr. Pibb became Pibb Xtra all of a sudden with no explanation. But no. Instead, I was watching that Ford-Taurus-wreck-of-a-sporting-event. Now, everyone pile into the Durango. Pizza's on me.

"Right now, we're just having fun."

I have made the decision, in conjunction with my therapist, to repeat this to myself ad nauseum so that I do not get ejected from a children's sporting event (again). At the end of the season, I will host an elaborate end-of-season party catered by Chipotle.

"What's important is that you played hard."

Your athletic skills and prowess are as unimpressive as a public official throwing out the first pitch at a baseball game. If your life depended on your abilities at this sport, you would be dead as a doornail. I'm directing attention to your effort to preserve you, for however brief a time, from the crushing reality of your own mediocrity. Now let's go to Dick's Sporting Goods and spend too much money on personalized equipment.

"Nice work out there, kid!"

Today, I did not second-guess my decision to live vicariously through the athletic performance of youth. I will sleep soundly tonight with as much faith in the future as I have in Starbucks' consistency across locations.

A SATURDAY ITINERARY
FOR A MIDWESTERN
YOUTH ATHLETE

6:45 A.M.	Wake up. Fall back asleep.
7:05 A.M.	Wake up again to an adult yelling: "It's go time. We're burning daylight!"
7:07 A.M.	Start getting dressed.
7:10 A.M.	Ask/yell: "Does anybody know where my shorts are?"
7:11 A.M.	Response: "You were supposed to put them in the dryer last night."
7:12 A.M.	Yell back: "I *did* put them in the dryer last night, somebody musta moved 'em."
7:13 A.M.	Find the shorts rolled up in the bottom of your gym bag.
7:14 A.M.	Yell: "Found 'em." No response.
7:15 A.M.	Go to the kitchen. Reject whatever breakfast is offered because you want a Croissan'wich from Burger King.
7:20 A.M.	Get in the car without your water bottle.
7:27 A.M.	Blast pump-up music in your earbuds while your parent orders your Croissan'wich.
7:29 A.M.	Finish Croissan'wich.
7:30 A.M.—7:50 A.M.	Drive to first game of the day.
7:50 A.M.	Blow past tournament check-in to warm up while the adults check their pockets for the entrance fee.
7:50 A.M.—8:00 A.M.	Warm up.
8:00 A.M.	During the pregame team meeting, motion to the stands that you need a water bottle. Ignore the eye roll as your adult stalks off to pay $2.50 for an Aquafina at the concession stand.
8:00 A.M.—9:00 A.M.	Play Game 1.
9:00 A.M.—9:10 A.M.	Change shoes.
9:15 A.M.	Leave your water bottle behind.
9:16 A.M.—10:30 A.M.	Go to Panera. Eat a bagel and a muffin.
10:45 A.M.	Go back to the tournament. Check in. Ask for money to buy a Gatorade.
10:45 A.M.—11:00 A.M.	Change shoes.
11:00 A.M.—12:00 P.M.	Play Game 2.
12:00 P.M.—12:20 P.M.	Change shoes.

12:30 P.M.—1:30 P.M.	Go to Chipotle. Eat a full burrito bowl, an order of chips plus guac, and a large soda.
1:30 P.M.	Return to the tournament. Ask for money to buy a bottle of water because they're out of cold Gatorade, except orange.
1:35 P.M.—1:50 P.M.	Change shoes.
2:00 P.M.—3:00 P.M	Play Game 3.
3:00 P.M.—3:30 P.M.	Change shoes.
3:30 P.M.—3:35 P.M.	Check the tournament bracket to see when your next game is. Fight with teammates about who your opponent will be.
3:40 P.M.—4:30 P.M.	Go to the nearest mall or Dave & Buster's. Split mozzarella sticks with the team. Order a burger, fries, and a milkshake. Spend $20 playing the arcade version of your sport before giving up and just doing the racecar thing or DDR.
4:45 P.M.	Return to the tournament. Cold Gatorade is back. Get blue.
4:47 P.M.—4:49 P.M.	Change shoes (you're running late!).
4:50 P.M.	Yell at your parents for saying they kind of hope you lose because then you wouldn't have another game until tomorrow.
4:52 P.M.	Tell your teammates you actually wouldn't mind losing because then you won't have to play until tomorrow and you guys could, like, go bowling or something.
6:00 P.M.	Win Game 4.
6:00 P.M.—6:40 P.M.	Change shoes.
6:45 P.M.—7:15 P.M.	Go to Chipotle again. Eat a whole burrito.
7:25 P.M.	Get back to the tournament. Fill up one of your empty water bottles at the drinking fountain because your parents refuse to spend another cent at that concession stand today.
7:26 P.M.— 7:59 P.M.	Change shoes.
8:00 P.M.—9:00 P.M.	Play Game 5.
9:00 P.M.—9:05 P.M.	Ask if your teammates can spend the night. Get immediately shot down.
9:05 P.M.	Take off your shoes and walk to the car in your socks.
9:10 P.M.	Hit McDonald's drive-thru for a 10-piece McNuggets.
9:15 P.M.—9:40 P.M.	Head home while reassuring your parents that you don't really have *that* much homework and it's not *that* big a deal, so it's fine if you have another tournament next weekend.
9:40 P.M.	Promise you'll put your uniform in the laundry.
9:42 P.M.	Put your dirty uniform in your bag.
9:45 P.M.—9:55 P.M.	Shower.
10:00 P.M.	Go to sleep (even though you're a little hungry).

College Sports

Consistently reminding yourself and everyone around you that they're young and it's just a game.

"That kid is special, huh?"

My adulation and adoration are all-consuming. I know more about the eating and sleeping habits of this nineteen-year-old phenom than I know about my own gastrointestinal health. My infatuation exhilarates me, but it also scares me, like all the shake options at Steak 'n Shake. If I ever saw them in public, I would nod politely and move on.

"They've really gotta get it together."

I spend at least one-third of my waking moments thinking about the lives and routines of college students. I genuinely believe that if I were put in a room with this team for two hours, I could turn this season around. When they graduate, I will fully sob.

"I think they're starting to get in sync."

Hope. It hangs, elusive but visible, just out of my reach.

"He's got a year of eligibility left."

I hope he stays. I hope he stays. I hope he stays. I hope he stays. I hope he stays. I hope he stays. But also, I want what's best for him and his family, so if he needs to declare, I—someone who's never interacted with him in my life—would understand and support him.

Professional Sports

Consistently reminding yourself that it's just a game.

"That kid is special, huh?"

My adulation and adoration are all-consuming. I know more about the eating and sleeping habits of this twenty-five-year-old phenom than I know about my own financial health. My infatuation exhilarates me, but it also scares me, like the depth and breadth of a Cheesecake Factory menu. If I ever saw them in public, I would nod politely and move on.

"Didja see the game last night?"

We do not have a lot in common, so I am most comfortable in conversations where we are either exchanging opinions about our hometown team or recapping their latest performance. I will insist that we go to/watch the next one together. First Bud Light's on me.

"We gotta get somethin' going soon."

It's starting to make less and less sense for me to be still watching this game. Unless the momentum begins a forward trajectory, it's going to be hard to justify not putting my energy toward "productive" tasks. Every time I mention that we need to pick it up soon, the clock on that futility restarts. I will now order or open another drink.

"It's a rebuilding year."

If I didn't continue to reassure myself of this, I would end every single day sobbing in my bed. I tell myself that it's worth it for the reduced ticket price and the pride of being a loyal fan, but my hair is falling out and my doctor is concerned. Last night, I couldn't even finish my Panera. And it was just soup! No bread bowl! Tomorrow, I will call all my friends and invite them to watch the next game from my box seats that I got half-off.

"I'm real proud of that team."

For decades hence, I will think of this moment and tear up. My life will forevermore be punctuated by my marriage, the birth of my children, the day the Super Target opened less than a mile away, and this game.

"That one hurt."

I was physically in pain the entire time. It is taking everything within me not to burst into tears at this moment. I have been to funerals that upset me less than what I just witnessed. Tonight, I'll seek my refuge at the bottom of a Dairy Queen Blizzard, a bag of Sonic Jumbo Popcorn Chicken, or three cans of Miller Lite. Tomorrow, I'll wear our team colors proudly into my place of work.

Michigan

NICKNAME: "The Great Lakes State"

REASON: . . . because the Great Lakes.

Sorry, that was rude. Four of the five great lakes (Superior, Michigan, Huron, and Erie) border the state of Michigan. The state itself is also great at having lakes, there are more than 11,000 of 'em.

WHAT EVERYONE THINKS THE CAPITAL IS: Detroit

ACTUAL CAPITAL: Lansing

FAMOUS MICHIGANDERS

Henry Ford	Lily Tomlin	Magic Johnson
Kristen Bell	Madonna	Smokey Robinson

FAMOUS PEOPLE WHO SPENT TIME IN MICHIGAN, SO IT COUNTS

Lucille Ball	Sojourner Truth
Rosa Parks	Thomas Edison

Auto industry
More than two million cars are produced in Michigan every year.

Detroit-style pizza
New York and Chicago can go 'round and 'round about their pizzas as much as they want, but Detroiters prefer to go *rectangle*. This edgier pie is thick, crispy, and chewy with Wisconsin brick-cheese right on the dough and tomato sauce on top of that. Some might be tempted to call it Sicilian-style pizza but, respectfully, what the heck are ya talkin' about? The real difference with Detroit-style pizza is the big ol' steel pan they cook it in. Legend has it that the first ever Detroiter 'za was made in a pan from a factory that was used for storing spare parts.

World's largest suspension bridge

Happy animals
Cage-free, baby! The Detroit Zoo was the first zoo in America to let animals roam more freely in open, spacious enclosures.

Michigan vs. Michigan State

Baby food   Breakfast cereal   Motown Records

Weekends off (aka the five-day workweek)
Union workers in the auto industry fought to get two days off, and now we all get weekends to sit outside and complain about having to go back to work!

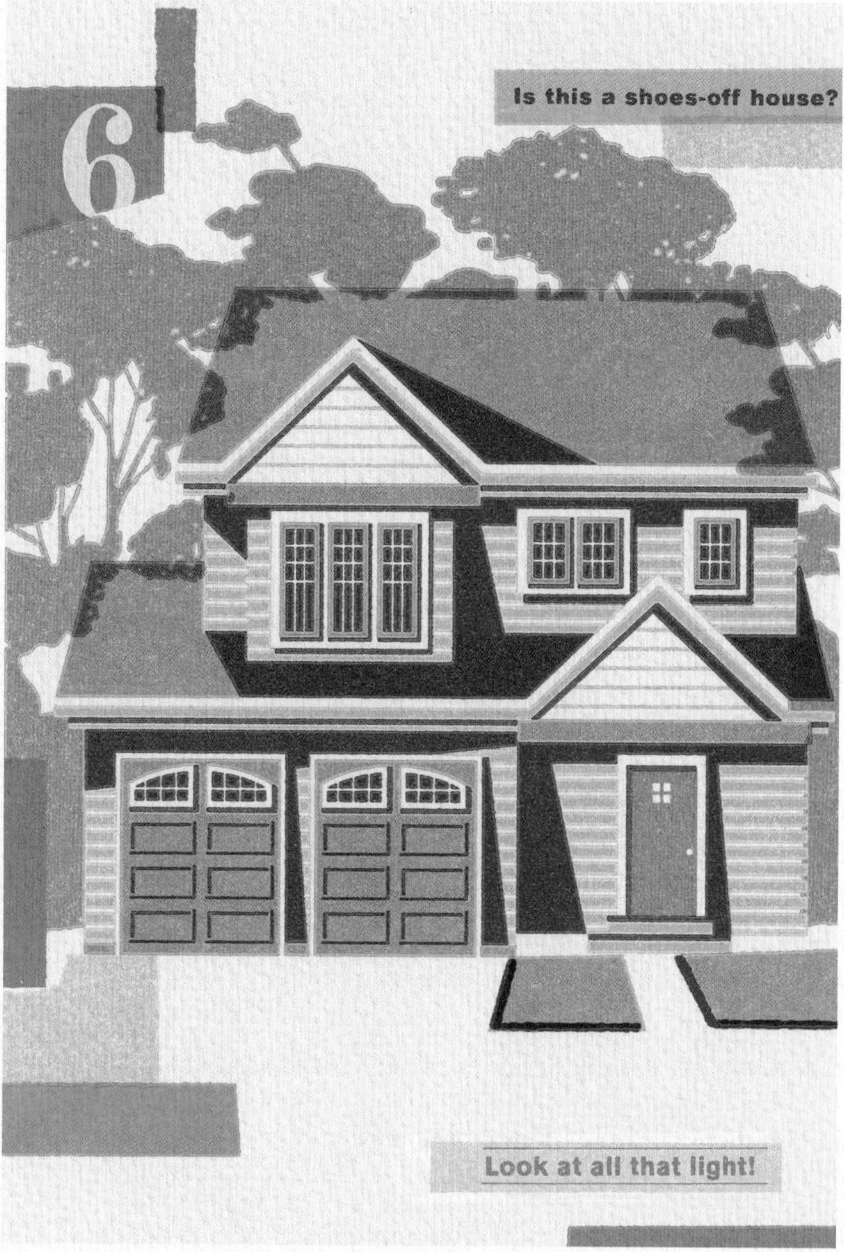
6
Is this a shoes-off house?
Look at all that light!

Home

For many Midwesterners, the home is the center of the action. It's where we cook out, host Thanksgiving dinner, snap prom pictures, and freak out about whether the house is presentable enough for serving Thanksgiving dinner or taking prom pictures.

As you humbly show off your own Midwestern abode, be sure to find the proper combination of pride and apology when guiding guests through each room. The tour should include not only details about what the visitors are currently seeing but also any and all plans you have to change the scenery—whether they're actual goals already set in motion or something that you saw in a Pottery Barn catalog last night. Remember, in a Midwestern home, the grand and the cute are of equal importance. So, while you're drawing people's attention to your new sliding glass door, don't forget to also point out that precious little bowl you got at an art fair last year from a woman who used to be a banker but gave it all up to make pottery—*idn't* that sweet!

When commenting on a Midwesterner's home, remember to always mention the yard, porch, natural light, and any piece of art that looks like it might have a personal story that the homeowner can tell you (see previous, re: banker/potter). If you're visiting as a part of a couple or a group, use loud conversations with those around you to really show your delight with every room, view, and item.

More than anything, the Midwestern home is a place to gather and share: food, stories, company, and tips for how to get a red-wine stain out of couch fabric. Because no matter who you give the credit to, it was a Midwesterner who said,

"There's No Place Like Home."

Hosting Guests at Your Home

Giving a tour, getting everyone a drink, and going on and on about how you're going to renovate in the fall.

"Just leave your shoes in the mudroom."
> Just leave your shoes in the place where you're currently standing, which I call a mudroom.

"Just leave your shoes in the sunroom."
> Just leave your shoes in the place where you're currently standing, which I call a sunroom.

"Just leave your shoes in the front hallway."
> Just leave your shoes in the place where you're currently standing, which I call the front hallway.

"Just leave your shoes in the foyer."
> Just leave your shoes in the place where you're currently standing; I was born on the East Coast or in Europe.

"On or off, up to you!"
> The house is getting cleaned tomorrow.

"Please forgive the mess."
> I've been cleaning up for the last hour and a half, but I'm covering my bases in case I've missed anything or this doesn't meet your standards of tidiness.

"Would you guys like the tour?"
(alternative: "Let me give you guys the tour.")
> I spent the last two days cleaning my home from top to bottom to perfectly curate the tour experience that you are about to receive. My self-worth is directly contingent on how many times you say, *"Oh, look at that,"* and *"Well, idn't that just gorgeous"* in the next four minutes.

"We don't spend nearly enough time in here, to be honest."

I forget this room exists, daily. When we first moved in, I had delusions of grandeur about spending so much luxurious time in this space. Now I only come in here to dust when guests are coming over and to wrap host gifts.

"We're doing some projects on the house, right now."

I have completely gutted the inside of my home. I enter my front door with a hard hat, and the sound of a power sander wakes me earlier than any rooster could ever dream. It costs more money, time, and hours of sleep than I could have imagined, but I paid good money* for this house, and I want a kitchen island if it kills me and my contractor (to whom I bring coffee and doughnuts every morning).

* I have neglected to include the Midwestern definition of "good money" out of respect for the minds and hearts of my East and West Coast readers. Please don't google it. For your own good.

"It's been a few years, so she's a little worse for wear."

It is dangerous for anyone to be in this house for longer than five minutes, let alone live here. I have a standing phone call with my life insurance company just to make sure that my affairs are taken care of when the Big One comes. At this point, it would be easier to just move. Once I fix her up, I'll have the whole neighborhood over for a housewarming party.

**"I'm thinkin' of taking out that wall there.
Open up the room a little bit."**

I went over to a neighbor's who had done the same thing and I can't stop thinking about it. What was once my dream home is now a hopelessly subpar temporary living space. I will not rest until this salon is spacious enough to host elaborate White Elephant gift exchanges and pre-prom photo sessions with the entire high school basketball team.

"It's almost time to start decorating for the fall!"

Hold on to your hats. I spend nine months of the year getting ready for these three months. I threw out my child's baby clothes so I could fill our entire keepsake closet with fall-leaf garlands, multicolored gourds, and little stuffed animals that hold up the chalkboards where I write "FALL in love" in perfect calligraphy. (I took a class at the community center!) This is my Olympics. My American Royal. My Grand Finale of Season 243 of *The Voice*. If I see someone whose home is inadequately ornamented, I will invite them to help themselves to my closet.

"Recognize this?"

I've been waiting to bring you here since the moment you stepped into my home. This is a significant object from our shared past, a gift you gave me, or something that I personally believe to be famous. Please find it as cool as I do. Regardless of whether you remember, I will tell the story, loudly and with gusto, of how I came to have this item. If you appear to like it, I will work tirelessly to get you one as well.

"It's got a nice, big garage."

That garage can fit your car(s), bikes, scooters, dog toys, old dollhouses, sports equipment, recycling bins, donations for The Goodwill from two years ago, power tools, gardening tools, Christmas presents you don't want the kids to see, broken appliances, trash bins, that broken TV that you know you have to throw out some special way but you don't know what it is and it's not causing anyone any trouble there anyway, and The Garage Fridge.

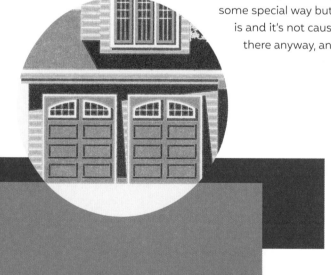

ODE TO
The Garage Fridge

'Twixt the SUV and recycling bin

Stand you with those two doors, upright and tall

Prepared to preserve all the goods put in

'Cause there's no way the house fridge fits it all

On game day when we're out of Miller Lites

Or a teen boy brings his whole entourage

For pop, Cool Whip, or extra Bagel Bites

We call upon you: fridge in the garage

The stable home of every ICEE Freeze

More eggs when the whole kitchen carton's done

An arsenal of nine bags of string cheese

Left over from the last big Costco run

Oh, shelter of the extra sliced turkey

Oh, keeper of that weird stuff Grandma made

With drawers full of Shasta and beef jerky

And one six-pack of Mike's Hard Lemonade

Life without you? Never, box of wonder

So many SunnyDs would go to waste

Premade pies and Hungry-Man's asunder

No oven-ready quiches would we taste

Garage fridge, how could I ever thank you

For all you do and store and keep and hold

I never thought I'd feel a warmth so true

For shelves and drawers that keep my groceries cold

Finished Basements

Ah, the finished basement. The hallmark of a Midwestern homeowner's domain. A sacred, carpeted space where young children can have sleepovers and build forts, and teens can play truth-or-dare as an excuse to make out with each other while someone watches the door (with those carpeted stairs, it's really hard to hear footsteps).

For adults, the finished basement is a sanctuary for watching TV after the kids go to bed, an escape from parties for an intimate conversation with people you actually like, or a sneaky parental trap to catch your kids making out (with those carpeted stairs, it's really hard to hear footsteps).

As far as all the bells and whistles on the finished basement (FB), each Midwestern house has its own distinct personality. When you descend into the FB, evaluate the choices of your hosts. Are they a pool-table family? A Ping-Pong household? An "entire separate kitchen and bedroom in case one of the in-laws becomes a regular fixture around here" abode? Is it a sports-worship den? A deity-worship den?

When embarking on your own FB project, think about the types of activities you want to take place in your own subterranean salon. Do you want it to be a hang-out spot? Invest in a comfy couch. A game-day go-to? Splurge on memorabilia and beer fridges (after you purchase the 4K big screen).

Of course, some FBs are vast enough to accommodate multiple themes or identities. Whether you're evaluating a friend's endeavor or building one of your own, never forget that it will always be the first place where kids will look for hidden presents, and if you hide gifts here and they're found, that is 100 percent on you.

More finished basement options

- Storage room masquerading as an art studio

- Big, serious study

- Craft room

- Exercise room

- Gift-wrap room

- Kiddo playroom

Visiting Someone Else's Home

Going on the tour, commenting on the decor, and figuring out which host gift you should bring next time.

"I can't believe it took us so long to get over here!"

I'm sorry, I'm sorry, I'm sorry. I know you kept inviting us and we kept being busy and it's totally our fault, but we really didn't know if it was going to be worth it. Now that we do, we'll come way more often! With presents!

"Ooooh, and it's got a porch!"

Please invite me over to drink wine and talk about the great sale they're having right now at Ann Taylor while we watch the sunset on this glorious porch. I will bring too much wine and leave the unopened bottles here!

"Now what's this over here?"

This caught my eye, and I am interested in an in-depth explanation of the object and, hopefully, a fascinating story. I also suspect I may be opening up an avenue for you to share a significant accomplishment that you or your family has achieved, which I will be able to use throughout the evening as a conversational tentpole! I hope you prove me right!

"Hon, come look at this. Idn't this neat?"

I love this so much. I want you, my spouse, to know that it's something I love, so you can get me something like it for the next gift-oriented holiday. Or I'll buy it for myself and you can wrap it.

— or —

Our host seems very excited about this object/decorating choice, and I want to match their enthusiasm so they don't feel embarrassed. I expect your demonstrated emotion to be about 2.5 times greater than your actual emotion.

"Well, just look at all these decorations! You really went all out!"

Did a pumpkin patch throw up in here? Everywhere I step unleashes a new fresh hell of autumnal nonsense. No one person should have this much time or disposable income to spend on turning a home into an orchard owner's wet dream. The next time I come over, I'll bring a gourd in the color that I notice you're missing.

"Oh, and just look at all that light!"

Any jealousy or resentment that I feel about your unfettered access to the sun has evaporated in the presence of such joyful and peaceful illumination. When I go home this evening, I will scour my house for south-facing walls and make plans to install new windows so that I, too, may know the glory of natural light. If you give me the name of your contractor, I'll send you a personalized basket from my gift closet.

"I just cannot get over these!"

I adore this facet of your home and will be talking about it incessantly for at least three months. Any time anyone tells me they have visited you, I will mention and fawn over these [paintings/plates/windows/etc.] until everyone's eyes glaze over. They will definitely be incorporated into my next host gift for this household.

STATE PROFILE
Minnesota

NICKNAME: "Land of 10,000 Lakes"

REASON: They have a lot of lakes!
The real number is actually closer to 14,000.

WHAT EVERYONE THINKS THE CAPITAL IS: Minneapolis

ACTUAL CAPITAL: St. Paul

FAMOUS MINNESOTANS

Bob Dylan	F. Scott Fitzgerald	Sinclair Lewis
Charles M. Schultz	Judy Garland	Walter Mondale
The Coen Brothers	Prince	

CLAIMS TO FAME

Juicy Lucy burger
A cheeseburger, but instead of the cheese on top, it's stuffed *inside* the patty, creating a melty, gooey, and, yeah, juicy center. Perfect idea. No notes.

Mall of America
There's a roller coaster in the mall! Inside! The! Mall! How 'bout that!?

Minnesota State Fair

First library with a dedicated children's section

Mississippi River starts at Minnesota's Lake Itasca

Princess Kay of the Milky Way
Every year, the Minnesota State Fair hosts the Minnesota Dairy Princess Program. This competition selects the next goodwill ambassador for the Minnesota dairy industry. The winner's official title is Princess Kay of the Milky Way. But the winners and finalists get more than just titles and PR obligations, they also get a bust of their head carved in, what else, butter.

IN-STATE CONFLICT

Matt's Bar vs. the 5-8 Club
Two bars within three miles of each other on the same street in Minneapolis are still duking it out over where the Juicy Lucy (the perfect cheeseburger where the cheese is, ingeniously, in the middle of the patty) was actually invented.

Pronto Pup vs. Corn Dog

YOU CAN THANK MINNESOTA FOR

Masking tape and transparent cellophane tape

Pop-up toaster

Rollerblades

Target!

It's not so bad without the wind

Weather

If Midwestern weather is a strange beast, then conversation about Midwestern weather is the zookeeper responsible for monitoring, caring for, responding to, and discussing the beast with everyone all over the world. Not only is weather our preferred conversation topic at the beginning and end of most interactions, it's also a valuable source of entertainment, scorn, and confusion. Midwesterners love to talk as much about what the weather *isn't* as what it actually *is*.

When we enter buildings, we comment on the weather. When we leave meetings, we anticipate the weather. When we sign emails, we encourage friends and colleagues to handle the weather (Stay warm! Keep cool out there!). For many of us, every Wednesday at 9 a.m. when the tornado sirens get tested, we're reminded that we live at the epicenter of violent but visually *super awesome* weather. One-way ticket to Tornado Alley, please.

If Coasties ask (and they always ask), we do get four seasons and we love to complain about all of them equally while pointing out that they "wouldn't be that bad" if the central tenet of their existence would just disappear: "It's not so bad without the humidity!" or "It's not so bad without the wind!"

An important thing to remember about conversing with Midwesterners about the weather is that most of us physically encounter it for five to seven minutes a day; the rest of the time, we watch it out the window. The fact that we mostly feel the cold or humidity or the wind or ice only as we rush from the doors of our cars to the door of the store or office does not exempt us from acting as though we've just walked fifteen blocks uphill both ways in the elements.

"Pretty hot"	90°F <
"Little warm"	80° to 90°F
"Real nice"	45° to 80°F
"Not too bad"	35° to 45°F
"A little nippy"	25° to 35°F
"Chilly"	15° to 25°F
"Pretty chilly"	0° to 15°F
"Pretty cold, not gonna lie to ya"	< 0°F

"Little chilly out there today."

I froze my freakin' nards off walking from my car to the front door. What heinous sins must we have committed to deserve this punishment from whatever God has wrought this blistering icy hell upon us? When we leave, I will stand outside holding the door as every single person exits the building.

"It's not so bad without the humidity."

When I am drenched in sweat, feeling like someone sprayed me with a garden hose full of Wild Cherry Pepsi, I try to imagine a world in which I am not covered in the sticky syrup of nature's pique. It is this self-delusion that guides me, sustains me, each moment I set foot outside my air-conditioned home or the well-cooled sanctuary of Trader Joe's. I now pass this self-deception on to you, along with an invitation to swim in my neighborhood pool whenever you want. I'll text you the gate code.

"It's not so bad without the wind."

It is cold and terrible outside. We are all kidding ourselves. Why do we live here? When will it end? I'm going to the store to buy a Duraflame Firelog value pack and then I'm not leaving my living room for the next three months except to go buy more ground beef and boxed brownie mix from the Hy-Vee.

"Cold enough out there for ya?"

You look terrible and frozen. Let me get you a hot chocolate.

"Hot enough out there for ya?"

You look terrible and sweaty. Let me get you a lemonade.

"We're getting a thunderstorm tonight."

Hell yeah! Do you see those freakin' clouds up there!? *Bang*, man, *Bang!* It's gonna be awesome. My Ford F-150 is in the garage, so I ain't thinking about hail. Or, more accurately, I am thinking about how I want the hail to be as big as golf balls so I can go "*Wow*, would ya look at that!" I bought the floor-to-ceiling windows in my house *specifically* to sit in My Good Chair and watch thunderstorms. As soon as I hear that first crack of thunder, I am outta here and into my chair. If anything happens to your car, though, just let me know. I know a good hail guy.

"It's really comin' down out there."

I'm going to google "can you drown standing up?" to ease my mind before I go back outside. Has someone checked on the oceans? 'Cause I think all the water in the world is in this twenty-mile radius right now. Good thing I keep a dry sweatshirt in a waterproof bag in my car. Do you want it?

"Wow, would ya look at that."

I stand in unfettered awe at the vastness and power of the natural world. The sky and land that stretch before us now make me fearful yet proud. Tonight, as I lie down to sleep, I will meditate on my own insignificance while I eat Boy Scout popcorn and watch *Friends* reruns on Nick at Nite. Would you like some of the popcorn? We bought extra.

"I'm gettin' eaten alive out here."

These damn bugs are driving me nuts. Here, take the last of my bug spray.

"That's all the jacket you got?"

Are you stupid? Do you not know how to dress yourself for the elements or is this some weird Freudian power play holdover from your youth? You should be as embarrassed for yourself as I am to be seen with you. In ten minutes, I will insist on giving you my car coat.

"Should be gettin' some sun soon."

We have to be, right? Like, come on. How much longer must we endure this dreary, cruddy nightmare of an outside? I hope that if I predict the sun's presence enough times, it will have to just go ahead and show up. Like when Miss Emma from next door says, "I can't wait to see you at the potluck," even though I already told her I had plans, and then, before you know it, I'm makin' a hot dish and going through the gift closet for a hostess gift.

"There she is."

SUN. SUN. SUN. SUN. SUN! I love you, the sun! I will find every possible excuse to go outside for the rest of the day. Do you need to borrow my backup pair of sunglasses?

"Did you guys see that double rainbow last week?"

I have twenty-seven blurry pictures of it on my phone, and I am going to show them all to you, no matter what you say.

"Sure do hope the weather cooperates with us."

Jesus God in heaven, can't we have *one* nice thing? I've been talking to my dog about this event for weeks! If it gets canceled, I will break into full sobs while I invite everyone over for ribs.

"How 'bout this weather?"

It's so nice outside I want to run around naked and roll around in the freshly sprinklered grass. I will now invite all my neighbors to have a sit-down on my porch.

"Looks like a tornado's comin'."

Grab the binoculars. Turn on the news. Put out the best snacks and sodas in the basement. Life is worth living again.

"Welp, we'd better head on down to the basement."

No way in hell are we missin' this. I will stand at the window and watch this tornado until I am literally choosing between my life and one more glimpse of the clouded, funnel-shaped mistress of darkness. If anyone's home is damaged in the storm, I'll obviously lead a citywide support drive. But *tomorrow*.

A NOTE ON

Tornado Alerts

WATCH means that environmental factors, actual or anticipated, make it likely for a tornado to occur.

WARNING means either that a tornado could materialize at any moment or that a tornado has already been sighted.

To summarize

WATCH means watch from the front window.

WARNING means watch from the basement window.

Missouri

NICKNAME: "The Show-Me State"

REASON: No one knows for sure.

There are two competing origins for Missouri's "Show-Me State" moniker. One story claims that it is a reference to Missouri's stubborn and noble skepticism in the face of government sweet-talking. "Don't just tell me what you're going to do, show me!" The other tale paints a slightly different picture, crediting the phrase to Missourians during the Gold Rush who were so out of their element that they had to consistently request tutorials for how to do absolutely everything. "I'm from Missouri . . . you're gonna have to show me."

WHAT EVERYONE THINKS THE CAPITAL IS: St. Louis

ACTUAL CAPITAL: Jefferson City

FAMOUS MISSOURIANS

Edwin Hubble	Gillian Flynn	Josephine Baker
Ellie Kemper	Harry Truman	Mark Twain
George Washington Carver	Jon Hamm	

FAMOUS PEOPLE WHO WERE TECHNICALLY BORN IN KANSAS (BUT WHO MISSOURI CLAIMS ANYWAY)

Charlie Parker

Ernest Hemingway   **Walt Disney**

CLAIMS TO FAME

Gateway Arch   **Kansas City–style barbecue**   **Lake of the Ozarks**

LITTLE-KNOWN CLAIM TO FAME

New Madrid Earthquakes of 1811–1812 in New Madrid (pronounced New MAD-rid), Missouri.
A series of three earthquakes (and thousands of aftershocks), each ranking in the top 20 largest earthquakes in US history and ranging from magnitude 6.7 to 8.8.

BIGGEST EARTHQUAKE THAT NEVER HAPPENED IN THE UNITED STATES

New Madrid, Missouri, December 3, 1990
In 1990, a self-proclaimed climatologist named Iben Browning predicted that an absolutely ginormous earthquake would level New Madrid and ring church bells all the way to Maryland. News crews and seismologists flocked to the small town of about 1,600 people to witness the destruction. But nothing happened. Oops!

IN-STATE CONFLICT

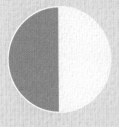

Half of the state calls it MissourUH.   **The other half of the state hates it when anyone calls it MissourUH.**

YOU CAN THANK MISSOURI FOR

Ice-cream cones (popularized)   **Iced tea (popularized)**   **Pancake mix**

Shopping

Shopping in the Midwest is a tightrope walk of socializing, sale-hopping, and strutting your stuff for friends and strangers alike. Midwesterners are #blessed to have a wide range of locales from which to choose in their shopping adventures, from classic mall retailers (and outlets) to garage and yard sales to the heartland's HomeGoods away from home, discount department stores. We're all Maxxinistas here.

The shopping conversations of the oceanless oasis revolve around addressing fellow shoppers' choices and questions with kindhearted honesty and savvy forward-thinking. A Midwesterner never just shops for today. They shop for that thing next month, stocking the gift closet, getting something because it's too cheap not to, and remembering right in the moment that Rebecca's son's graduation is next weekend and do we have anything for that or know his size?

Shopping is also a communal experience, and not just because the odds of seeing someone you already know on your shopping trip are higher than the Gateway Arch. When you step out of a dressing room or hold a cute coffee mug that says, SHHH . . . THERE'S WINE IN HERE, you are walking into a world of compliments and reassurances from everyone around you. They may even point you in the direction of a similarly "so stinkin' cute" item marked *Clearance!*

As you converse and traverse the racks or yard-sale tables with your companion, remember that between the attic, basement, storage room, and gift closet, there is space for everything. All that matters is finding something that's "a steal" that "you can't live without" or that "would make a great gift for that thing."

"Can I help you folks find anything?"

I know people hate being asked this question, and that our handbook requires it causes me physical pain. If I had my way, all the sales associates would be sitting in comfy chairs in the back waiting to be summoned by whoever needs us and otherwise leaving you all the eff alone. But I have to pay for my QuikTrip Cherry Sprite habit somehow, and as long as it's with this retail job, I've just gotta go with the flow. If you're not super-rude to me, I'll go nuts and let you combine coupons at checkout.

"We're just looking, thanks!"

Please don't follow us around the store and try to sell us stuff. Being tailed by a sales associate and unable to shake them gives me more anxiety than driving my ten-year-old Ford Fusion on the interstate. I will go online and name you specifically in a positive review.

"Oh, I love your _____."

Please tell me where you got it, if it's comfortable, how much you paid for it, and whether it was on sale. I will then tell you that it looks great, specifically on you, and highlight which of your features it complements most.

"It's not doin' ya any favors."

Everything you don't like about the way you look is currently on unabashed display. I could not, in good conscience, let you even think about purchasing this item. I *will* levy constant compliments on you throughout the rest of this shopping trip.

"You don't think it's too . . ."

I'm not feeling perfect about this ensemble and am starting to get more self-conscious than a high school teacher running into their students at a music festival. I am going to need you to systematically compliment it and me for the rest of our time together. I will return the favor next week when you recommend a new bar.

"Imma get a couple for the gift closet."

I'm going to buy every single one in stock and then come back next week to see if there are more.

"Oh, this would be perfect for that thing!"

I want this item but it is not wearable every day, so I desperately need to justify my purchase! Whether or not I will wear it to "that thing" is irrelevant. I must have it. But first, I must have a reason to have it. Would you like the item next to it? I'm buying!

"I'll wait till it's on sale."

My need for this item is not immediate, and I consider paying retail to be a sign of weakness. I will now go purchase gifts from the "Just Arrived" section of this store.

"Do you think you'll wear it?"

I don't think you'll wear it. If you prove me wrong, I'll compliment it every time and call it a cute name, like "your Ruby Tuesday best."

"Listen to me. You look great."

This lack of confidence stops *now*. That outfit makes you look hotter than a grandma at an August soccer tournament. I won't have this hemming and hawing on my watch! I am already planning an event just so you can wear this in public.

"Well, isn't this just the cutest thing!"

I would sacrifice my left arm if it meant that I looked good in this item. I want it. I want it. I want it. I want it. If someone else grabs the only one in my size, I will let it go without a fight.

"If you like it, I like it."

It's absolutely disgusting, and I'm questioning every nice thought I've ever had about your taste in anything. Every time that I see it on you, I will squeal and say, "You were right—I love that on you more each time!"

"Oh my gosh, I love that one, I just bought it for my daughter."

You look lost and unsure and as alone in the world as a vegetarian at a pit barbecue. Obviously, it looks better on my daughter, but that's neither here nor there. When you're done, I'll ask you to stand in line with me so you can use my coupon.

"Oh, that's a steal."

I will buy as many of these as possible to gift to loved ones, while loudly and proudly announcing the price. It's not gauche if it's a steal!

"What do you think of this?"

I'm not sure if I love it or think it's the ugliest thing I've ever set eyes on, and I need someone else to weigh in so I know how I feel. I'll agree with whatever you say.

"Well, it's a little pricey isn't it?"

Eff this. I could make this with my own two hands and it would be way better. I don't understand how people actually spend money on this crap. I will recommend this store and item to my mother-in-law when she visits.

"I guess this is kind of what they're wearing now, isn't it?"

I hate this new style almost as much as I hate being confronted by the reality of my age. I know that people my current age felt the same way about the latest styles when I was younger, but this is different, right? Right? I know it's not different. In my heart, I know. But seeing today's youth in these new styles forces me to confront my mortality, and I can hardly stand it. The next time I see someone wearing the new style, I will say, "Look at you! So cute, so hip!"

"Doesn't [name] just need this!?"

I would not look good in this. You would not look good in this. But this would look good on *someone*, and I know who that someone is! I'm going to buy it right now, along with two pairs of cute socks I don't need.

"See anything you can't live without?"

I'm just about ready to wrap up this shopping trip.

"We good here?"

I am now fully ready to wrap up this shopping trip.

"Can we go?"

I was ready to wrap up this shopping trip ten minutes ago. Mentally, I am already on my porch with a glass of wine.

Shopping at a Garage/Yard Sale

Deciding whether to buy people's personal stuff without making it personal!

"Whadda they want for it?"

I want to know how much this item is, but I don't want to be the one to ask. Please obtain this information and report back.

"How much is this gonna set me back?"

I have an idea of an acceptable number in my head; if the price is within five dollars of that in either direction, I will purchase this thing. If the price is too high, I will purchase something else for my "acceptable" price—otherwise, I will feel bad.

"Whaddya got here?"

I think I understand what this table full of items is, but I have been to too many garage sales to believe my eyes at first glance. Once you confirm what exactly it is that I am looking at, I will decide whether this is a "purchase items" garage-sale trip or a "listen to fun stories and thoroughly wash my hands after" garage-sale trip.

"Quite the collection!"

Please regale me with whatever weird story brought this amount of [Beanie Babies/baseball cards/records/LEGO Minifigures/Madame Alexander dolls/Hot Wheels/salt and pepper shakers] into your possession, and why you have chosen this moment to sell them to your neighbors. I will remember this story forever and reference it every time we interact from this second forward.

"Idn't this cute?"

I want to talk about this item with someone, but I'm not sure that I want to purchase it. Let's go a few rounds back and forth listing other cute things it reminds us of and fun places to put it. If you end up liking it more than I do, I will buy it for you; no questions asked.

Nebraska

NEBRASKA
NE

NICKNAME: "The Cornhusker State"

REASON: Before the machinery was invented, Nebraskans used to husk corn with their hands!

WHAT EVERYONE THINKS THE CAPITAL IS: Omaha

ACTUAL CAPITAL: Lincoln

FAMOUS NEBRASKANS

Fred Astaire

Marlon Brando

Warren Buffett

Gerald Ford

Roxane Gay

William Jennings Bryan

Malcolm X

FAMOUS PEOPLE WHO SPENT TIME IN NEBRASKA, SO IT COUNTS

Willa Cather

Only state with a unicameral legislature

Only triply landlocked state in the United States

Runza sandwich
Known in other places as a bierock, krautburger, or kraut pirok, this cultural culinary staple features beef, onions, cabbage, and spices stuffed into a rectangular bread pocket. Yes, you can get a Runza sandwhich at one of the Runza restaurants in neighboring states such as Iowa and Kansas, but that's kind of like saying you can get Kansas City Barbeque in New York City: It's technically true, but false on a spiritual level.

World's largest ball of stamps

Only state with publicly owned utilities

Reuben Rivalry—Nebraska vs. New York
Do Nebraskans take their sandwiches seriously? You betcha! There are two competing stories from two competing states claiming to be the birthplace of the classic deli combo of corned beef, Swiss cheese, sauerkraut, and Russian dressing on two slices of rye. New York claims the sando was first concocted on 58th Street by deli owner Arnold Reuben. Nebraska insists that it was born in Omaha's Blackstone hotel when Bernard Schimmel whipped up one for a poker buddy, Ruben Kulafofsky (very Midwestern of Bernard to name it after someone else). Both places lay claim, but only Omaha has an actual menu from 1937 that lists "The Reuben" sandwich. Point to the cornhuskers!

CliffsNotes

911 emergency system

Kool-Aid

Omaha Steaks

Relationships

In the heartland, the heart wants what it wants. It also wants to talk about what all the other hearts want and whether it approves of the match, thinks one of them can do better, or saw them together once in the Jimmy John's parking lot and is curious if there's something going on.

Midwesterners flirt, date, fall in love, break up, and develop meaningful friendships just like the rest of the world. But for the most part, we do it with a strong awareness that we will most *definitely* be seeing these people again. Probably multiple times a year. Most likely in a Barnes & Noble or at someone's graduation.

We let out the real feelings with our closest friends; but in public and polite Midwestern conversation, we let our word choice do the talking. When it comes to weighing in on other people's relationships, Midwesterners employ the science of verbal winks accompanied by actual smirks and eyebrow raises.

Whether you're offering full-throated approval by calling someone "just a doll" or pledging to hate them forever by "wishing them the best," remember that whatever you say behind someone's back you'll end up repeating to their face while waiting for Broccoli Cheddar Soup in a bread bowl at Panera.

Talking About Your Relationships

How to gush, vent, and roll your eyes without doing any of those things. (You're in LOVE!)

"I don't really want to label anything yet."
> They like me more than I like them, but I might like them more later. If I do decide it's not working out, I will cook their favorite dinner and send them home with leftovers.

"We're not really putting labels on stuff."
> I am completely smitten but don't want to scare them off. This "no labels" thing is 100 percent not my choice, but I am pretending to be cool. I'd go to HomeGoods to start our registry right now. But I won't. Thanks for listening, and please let me buy the next round so I can gush more.

"We stayed up all night talking."
> I know I'm not supposed to say I'm in love already, but I'm absolutely head over heels. Every conversation you and I have for the next three weeks will be about my relationship with this person. I have already preordered your custom mug that says, WORLD'S MOST PATIENT FRIEND.

"We're probably just gonna go home and watch a movie or something."
> Teens: We're going to pick a movie that neither of us really cares about and make out on the sectional in my parents' finished basement.
>
> Adults: We're going to put on the movie that we've been trying to watch for two weeks and one of us is going to fall asleep in the middle.

"We're just having fun."
> Lots of sex. A bunch of sex. Just so much sex.

"I'm not sure we're on the same page."
> Stage! Five! Clinger! Holy moly. I must pretend to have IBS just to get some freakin' *air*. The texting is constant, the hand-holding is giving me

calluses, and the talking is more sticky-sweet than the vinaigrette dressing on Wendy's Strawberry Fields Salad. We're only still together because the nice restaurant (with tablecloths!) where I want to break up doesn't have a reservation until next week.

"Honestly, the breakup is a good thing."

I cannot stop crying. I frequently consider boarding a one-way flight to the desert so I can just sit there and let the sand take me. Someday, I'm sure, I will be able to move past the pain of this broken heart. Someday when I am dead. The next time I encounter my ex at a restaurant, I'll insist that they come share our table.

"We just wanted different things."

I wanted someone to be in a loving, adult relationship with me, and they wanted to bang everything that moved this side of the Mississippi. I wanted to go out for a nice dinner once in a while, and they wanted to burp the alphabet in my face with Panda Express breath. I wanted to go on walks along the local trail; they wanted to go to the youth soccer fields and pretend to be a drunk parent yelling at the high school ref. If they ask if they can use me as a reference for their next job, I'll agree.

Teen Romance

Teen romance in the Midwest is full of half-dates masquerading as group outings. Here's a quick primer on what's really in the hearts of our adolescent heartland heartbreakers.

"A few of us are going to Red Robin, do you want to come?"

I am romantically interested in you but not sure if you feel the same way, so I'm arranging a way for us to spend time together in a casual social setting. I will try to figure out a way to sit close to you and try to playfully steal your Campfire Sauce if you don't steal mine first.

"You're comin' to IHOP, right?"

The only reason I agreed to go with the rest of the kids in the school play was to be with you. I don't even like strawberry syrup that much! If you're not going, I will go, pretend to have a good time, and buy someone else's meal.

"Me and a few people are gonna go sit at the tables at Sonic, do you wanna come?"

I love you. Let's please sit on each other's laps all night and throw Tater Tots at each other as an excuse to grab hands.

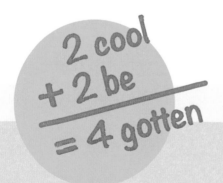

2 cool
+ 2 be
———————
= 4 gotten

Talking About Other People's Relationships

How to gush, vent, and roll your eyes without ever doing any of those things. (*They're* in love.)

"So . . . any updates?"

I have been checking my watch every seven minutes for the past two days waiting for updates on your latest romantic endeavor. I canceled a pretty necessary medical appointment in order to block out the requisite four hours for you to tell me everything that has happened and how you're feeling about it in painstaking detail. If you dodge the question, I will respectfully move on and text your sister about it when I get home.

"The most important thing is that you're happy."

I'll give it two months. (Obviously, you can sleep at my place through the whole breakup.)

"Have you met him/her yet?"

I don't want to cloud your judgment, but I want to gossip with you *so bad*!

"He's/she's nice."

4/10

"He's/she's a sweetheart."

6.5/10

"He's/she's just a doll."

11/10

"He's just adorable."

He is kind, a little bit shy, and sort of goofy. He acted interested in everything I said and gave me perfectly appropriate compliments that made me wish he was my son. He has cemented himself as the permanent recipient of either a "Hi, sweetheart, how are you?" or a "Hey, buddy, how's it going?"

"Moms love him."

He is a sweet, conscientious man who everyone kind of hated in high school.

"She's cute as a button."

I didn't get to talk to her very much but watching her glide around the room laughing and joking felt like I was watching a silent montage in a rom-com. When she said goodbye to me, it was like we'd spent the entire night together, just us, and it was the best evening she ever had, even though we didn't say more than ten words to each other. The next time I see her, I'll greet her like an old friend.

"I'm just so happy for them!"

Seeing them together restores my faith in humanity. If anything ever happens to either of them or their relationship, I will go into full-fledged Victorian mourning for three years.

"Good for her!"

She deserves the world, and it was the great agony of my life that I could not personally conjure a partner for her out of Diet Dr Pepper cans and gift soap. Tonight will be the first peaceful sleep I've had in months. I have already preordered a KitchenAid Stand Mixer as a wedding present.

— or —

I hate her and don't give a flying hoot about her happiness, but it's rude to hear about someone's good fortune without commenting in some way. I have already preordered a KitchenAid Stand Mixer as a wedding present.

— or —

Wow, that person is out of her league, and I doubt it's going to last. I have already preordered a KitchenAid Stand Mixer as a wedding present.

"Good for him!"

That he found a heart to love brings me unbridled joy. If a witch needed "a heart of pure gold" to create an elixir for eternal life, I would take his heart. We are unworthy of his pure goodness. He belongs in his own sanctuary with extra-soft sweatshirts and twenty-five-cent Wing Night. Next time I see him, I'll greet him with a huge hug and an "it's so great to see you happy, man."

— or —

Really? That guy? I mean, okay. I mean, everyone deserves love but . . . come on, *him*? One time I saw that dude throw up in the trunk of a Corolla and then do a keg stand. He made me watch *Field of Dreams* in German because "the acting transcends language." I just . . . you know what? Fine. Next time I see him, I'll greet him with a huge hug and an "it's so great to see you happy, man."

"Good for them!"

This is not going to end well.

"I wish him/her the best."

Damn them to hell.

"I think they'd been having some issues for a while."

Thank effing *God* that is *over*. Every single time I saw either of them, I got turned into a relationship therapist. Now I can finally enjoy a cup of Folgers on my porch without having moderately snippy text messages read aloud to me, so that I can say, "Oh yeah, that's not good," or "Hmm, so what are you going to do?" I have my *life back*! I sent both of them condolence cakes from Baskin-Robbins, and I have a scheduled happy hour at Houlihan's every other day for the next two weeks.

Non-Romantic Relationships

Talking to and about friends, coworkers, and friends of friends of coworkers.

"I feel like we never see each other nowadays."

> Are you mad at me? I feel like maybe you're mad at me and secretly running the other way every time you see me in the Noodles & Company parking lot. There is not a hot dish I wouldn't make or a flower arrangement I wouldn't send to get us back to the once-every-three-months interactions I value so much. Once we part ways, I will send three (3) well-spaced follow-up texts before giving up.

"We don't see as much of each other anymore."

> Social media posts indicate that they have truly fallen off the deep end, and I don't trust myself to be in the same room with them without bringing it up. Obviously, I will still send them our holiday newsletter.

— or —

> The last few times we saw each other things were stilted and awkward in a way that could not even be saved by talking about the weather, surrounding decor, or latest shenanigan of our mutual "fun friend." Obviously, I will still invite them to our holiday party.

"We've spoken a few times."

> He is either completely boring or an abhorrent excuse for a human being, but I have nothing further to say about him except that once or twice I was forced to acknowledge his existence in the form of stilted conversation. The next time I see him, I will graciously hug him.

"He has a tendency to be friendly."

> Bitch, run. But still wave to him in church. We're not animals.

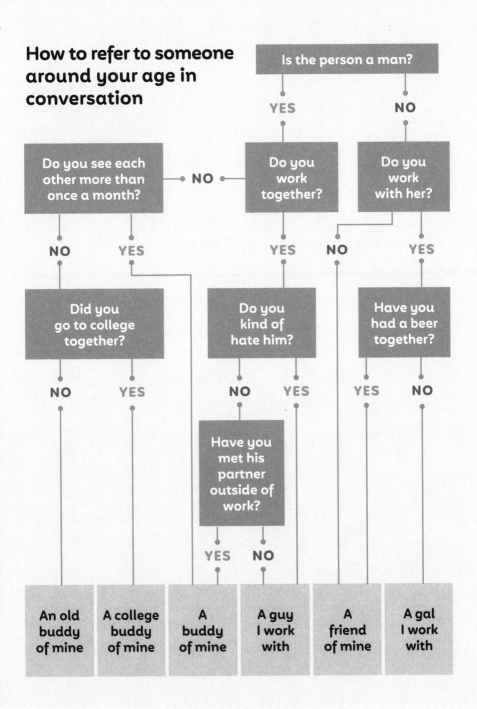

How to refer to someone around your age in conversation

North Dakota

NICKNAME: "The Peace Garden State"

REASON: It is home to part of the International Peace Garden, which sits on the border of the United States and Canada.

WHAT EVERYONE THINKS THE CAPITAL IS: Fargo

ACTUAL CAPITAL: Bismarck

FAMOUS NORTH DAKOTANS

Jay Gatsby	Lawrence Welk	Wiz Khalifa
Kellan Lutz	Marge Gunderson	

FAMOUS PEOPLE WHO SPENT TIME IN NORTH DAKOTA, SO IT COUNTS

Meriwether Lewis and William Clark
Their Corps of Discovery went through North Dakota twice over the course of their journeys; almost one-fourth of their expedition was spent in the state.

Phil Jackson   Ronda Rousey

CLAIMS TO FAME

Fargo (the movie)
Although no scenes from the Oscar-winning Coen Brothers movie were actually filmed in Fargo (bummer!), the Fargo-Moorhead Visitors Center is now home to the famous woodchipper used in the film.

Theodore Roosevelt National Park

World's largest french-fry feed

LITTLE-KNOWN CLAIMS TO FAME

The Mid-est of the Midwest!
Rugby, North Dakota, is the official geographical center of North America.

Record for most snow angels made simultaneously in a single location.

The United States of America's largest producer of honey. Sweet!

INTRA-STATE CONFLICT

Both North Dakota and South Dakota wanted to be the first Dakota admitted to the union. To make things fair, the president at the time, Benjamin Harrison, signed the papers without looking at the name so he wouldn't know which one he signed first. The announcements, however, were made alphabetically so North Dakota got the official win in the end.

YOU CAN THANK NORTH DAKOTA FOR

Cream of Wheat   **Mr. Bubble**

You guys from around here?

EXIT 132

8

Lemme get the lay of the land

Travel

For Midwesterners, *travel* is a broad and all-encompassing term. We travel within our hometowns to visit friends, throughout the Midwest to visit other equally ocean-free cities and towns, and outside the central twelve to see how the other 79 percent live.

Whether we're experiencing a new place ourselves or playing host for someone else's trip, the Midwestern travel doctrine stands firm: you can usually drive wherever you need to go, you're probably gonna wanna make a quick stop on the way there to check out that thing ya can't miss, and you don't need to know the exact address, just a few landmark-based directions will be A-okay.

We also like to comment on the terrain of anywhere we are, particularly the potholes and constant construction. In fact, there's a joke in every Midwestern burg that each town thinks it invented. "Here in [Town] we like to say we have two seasons: Winter and Construction." Please laugh like you've never heard it before. It's the Midwestern thing to do.

Whether you're "just popping in" to a new place or showing off your hometown to a new face, enjoy where you are, talk loudly about how great it is, and be sure to swing by whatever local spot "has, like, won awards and stuff."

"It's a pretty quick drive."

It is less than 4 hours.

"It's not too far a drive."

It is more than 5 hours but less than 10 hours.

"It's a bit of a drive."

It is a more than 10 hours but less than 20 hours.

"'Course you can drive it."

It is more than 20 hours.

"Now, you gotta fly to get there."

It is outside the continental United States.

"I don't know the address but I know how to get there."

Turn off Google Maps; I don't need any of that. You just drive past the
Buffalo Wild Wings—not that one, the other one. Then you turn right at
the high school where we saw that play the one time. Keep going until
ya get to the intersection with the angel statue. Then turn left and it's the
house with the squirrel sticker on the mailbox, right next to the house
with the bright pink door.

"Now watcha gonna wanna do is . . ."

Come, let me take you under my wing and bestow upon you the wisdom
that is "directions to a local landmark." There are things you need to know
about roads, people, and nice views that you aren't going to get from
anyone else. I guess that's not true, anyone else would probably also give
you the same wisdom. You know what, hop in the back seat of the Altima.
I'll just take ya.

"They gotta do somethin' about these roads."

Every time we drive here, I feel my genitals in ways that are counter to God's Plan. The condition of these streets is an affront to angels and architects alike. The only reason I even come to these godforsaken half trenches is to bring eighty-seven-year-old Miss Louisa the extra doughnuts from Tommy's every Sunday. I will never stop.

"I mean, can they leave us just one road to drive on?"

I understand that construction is necessary in order to avoid on-road genital distress. But also I hate construction and it is very inconvenient, and I am going to write a firmly worded letter to the city and deliver it with homemade puppy chow.

"We're just gonna pop in for a visit."

We will arrive and say our hellos while standing in the front hall for one and a half hours. Then we will relocate to the living room or the porch/yard, depending on the weather, and snack on mostly chips while we talk about families, work, and crazy stories from our youth for another two or three hours over the sounds of a game playing on TV. At some point, one of our hosts will offer to start up the grill and, based on our plans for the evening, we will either accept their invitation to dinner or kindly insist that we hate to but have to go. Regardless, goodbyes will be forty-five minutes to an hour. (For details on The Midwestern Goodbye, see page 131)

"You guys from around here?"

I noticed that your clothes are out of place and that you look more lost than a deer in a suburban subdivision. I'm interested in knowing more about where you're from and whether I should recommend my favorite fancy dinner place or a dive bar. Either way, I know the owner, she'll getcha a table.

"Oh yeah, I read about that place. It's won a couple of awards."

This [restaurant/retail store/cookie shop] has earned that coveted badge of "external approval"! We have to check it out so we can decide if it's worth the hype or if we're going to hold it up against our current, local favorite and find it wanting.

"I just need to get the lay of the land."

Everyone be quiet for a few moments so I can summon confidence and establish dominance over this new terrain. My ego is heavily wrapped up in having authority over physical locations, and as soon as I can attain a base comfort level, I can fake it until I make it for the rest of our trip. I am also trying to locate the nearest Sonic or comparable eatery because I am hungry but have not done research on restaurants and could not emotionally handle accidentally taking us some place that is not good.

"We're in town for a few days, anything we can't miss?"

I want to be able to forge strong human connection with anyone I meet from this area from this moment forward. Give me the stuff that people are going to ask me about when I tell them I visited here! The things that will impress people! The things I might actually enjoy. Then I will refer to you henceforth as "a lovely person named [your name]" in all my stories of your fair town.

"What do you guys do for fun around here?"

We booked the hotel and decided where to eat on the first night but those are literally all the plans we've made. Help. Tomorrow, I'll bring you a personalized gift from wherever you send us.

Meeting a Midwesterner

When someone says, "I'm from Illinois."

Instead of saying, "I've been to Chicago!"

Try, "What an honor to be speaking to someone from the state that gave us the Ferris wheel! Congrats on leading the nation in electricity production from nuclear power!"

When someone says, "I'm from Indiana."

Instead of saying, "Where even is that?"

Try, "Ah! The site of America's first professional baseball game. Thank goodness Indiana native Orville Redenbacher provided the snacks!"

When someone says, "I'm from Iowa."

Instead of saying, "Oh, so you grow potatoes?"

Try, "Wow, how does it feel to be on the front lines of democracy every four years? Thank you for John Wayne!"

When someone says, "I'm from Kansas!"

Instead of saying, "Oh, like Dorothy!"

Try, "Wow! Congrats on living in the state that invented the helicopter. I love what Kansas native and former president Dwight Eisenhower did with the interstate system!"

When someone says, "I'm from Michigan."

Instead of saying, "Show me on your hand!"

Try, "Move over, Michigan native Henry Ford, I'm trying to get to the casino, since Detroit is the largest American city to offer them! With all that earning potential, no wonder Michigan has the most registered snowmobiles in the nation!"

When someone says, "I'm from Minnesota."

Instead of saying, "*Minnesoooootah.*"

Try, "I can't wait to go to the Minnesota State Fair! I heard they carve an entire bust out of butter! Maybe they'll carve one of famous Minnesotan Prince."

When someone says, "I'm from Missouri."

Instead of saying, "Haha. Weird."

Try, "Good ol' Missouri! What a pivotal player in the westward expansion of our country! Don't you think it's a fun coincidence that Mark Twain was born right after an appearance of Halley's Comet *and* died the day after Halley's Comet appeared seventy-four years later? Folks probably saw the comet a lot better after Missourian Edwin Hubble created his eponymous telescope!"

When someone says, "I'm from Nebraska."

Instead of saying, "Do you live in a cornfield?"

Try, "Disputed birthplace of the Reuben sandwich and undisputed birthplace of Kool-Aid? Doesn't get much better than that, unless you enjoy them both on the world's largest covered porch swing, amirite?"

When someone says, "I'm from North Dakota."

Instead of saying, "Oh, I didn't know people actually lived there."

Try, "Someday I'd love to go to the world's largest french-fry feed! I'll be sure to take a lot of pictures on my Kodak camera, which was invented by a North Dakotan!"

When someone says, "I'm from Ohio."

Instead of saying, "I'm sorry."

Try, "How do you choose between all the wonderful ice-cream and museum offerings in your state! Jeni's, Graeter's, The Rock and Roll Hall of Fame, The American Classical Music Hall of Fame!? Making a selection is, as Ohioan Neil Armstrong would say, "one small step for man, one giant leap for mankind!"

When someone says, "I'm from South Dakota."

Instead of saying, "Why?"

Try, "Home to L. Frank Baum, Laura Ingalls Wilder, Sitting Bull, *and* Crazy Horse! Tell me more about the world's only Corn Palace!"

When someone says, "I'm from Wisconsin."

Instead of saying, "*Cheeeeesssee*, right!?"

Try, "What I wouldn't give to share a great glass of Wisconsin beer with Hattie McDaniel or Orson Welles. I wonder what they would have thought about the Packers being the only publicly owned, not-for-profit major professional sports team!"

STATE PROFILE

Ohio

NICKNAME: "The Buckeye State"

REASON

Initially: The prevalence of Ohio buckeye trees

Now: The Ohio State University Buckeyes and the delicious treat known as buckeyes, which is peanut butter fudge dipped in chocolate. Any questions?

WHAT EVERYONE THINKS THE CAPITAL IS: Cleveland

ACTUAL CAPITAL: Columbus

FAMOUS OHIOANS

Dave Grohl	LeBron James	Simone Biles
James Thurber	Neil Armstrong	Toni Morrison
John Glenn	Orville and Wilbur Wright	

CLAIMS TO FAME

Cuyahoga River fire of 1969	Pro Football Hall of Fame	Rock and Roll Hall of Fame

Skyline Chili

It's pretty simple. You take spaghetti or a hot dog and then ya slather it with chili and shredded cheddar cheese. Of course, the chili itself is made with a little somethin' special; a unique blend of [REDACTED].

US presidents—seven of them! Benjamin Harrison, James A. Garfield, Rutherford B. Hayes, Ulysses S. Grant, Warren G. Harding, William Howard Taft, William McKinley

US president William Henry Harrison wasn't born in Ohio but he lived here when he twice ran for and once was elected president. He is, sadly, perhaps most famous for delivering the longest presidential inauguration speech in history and then dying exactly one month later, setting the record for Shortest Presidential Term that still stands.

The actual invention of the airplane!

Yes, the Wright brothers first flew it in Kitty Hawk, North Carolina (that's why NC license plates say, "First in Flight"), but they *built* it in Ohio.

Graeter's vs. Jeni's vs. Mitchell's

Cincinnati's airport is actually in . . . *Kentucky*

Light bulbs

Superman

The creators of Superman, Jerry Siegal and Joe Schuster, met in high school in Cleveland!

Vulcanized rubber

I SAW THIS SIGN ON FACEBOOK AND BOUGHT IT

I WOULDN'T SAY THIS IN PUBLIC BUT I'll PUT IT ON A SIGN

★ ★ ★ ★ ★
I SUPPORT
A GUY I MET AT A BLOCK PARTY WHO SEEMED NICE AND REMEMBERED MY NAME

THIS SIGN SAYS TO MY NEIGHBORS WHAT I SHOULDN'T SAY TO THEIR FACES

Politics

Living in swing-state central means that all Midwesterners are virtually guaranteed, on an almost daily basis, to interact with people who have different politics. But do not mistake our civility for apathy. During election season, the yard signs come out and the gloves come off. But the neighborhood barbecues carry on.

"I don't really talk about politics too much."

I know what I think, and I don't really care what people have to say about it. I will now change the subject by giving a very specific and conscientious compliment to the quietest person in the room.

"Now, I understand it's a hard job, but . . ."

I could walk into [politician's] office holding my sick four-year-old (no iPad!) and get more done in three hours than those good-for-nothing invertebrates have done all year. If I ever see them in person, I will smile and say, "Thanks for all the hard work!"

"Hmm, now I'm not too sure that I agree with that."

You're an absolute moron and I don't really have the time to explain to you why 2 + 2 = 4, since all the educators in your life were apparently unsuccessful. I'll bow out of this conversation by inviting you to a barbecue in my backyard.

"That's interesting. More lemonade?"

The more time we spend on this subject, the closer you get to a grisly death and the closer I get to jail time. Since the obvious rising tension of the room wasn't enough to shut your French Silk Pie hole, I guess I'll have to redirect the conversation myself by bringing up our local sports team or asking you a question about your latest personal accomplishment.

"All I'll say is . . ."

Any time this topic comes up, I have my prepared statement at the ready. I have perfected this fifteen- to twenty-word masterpiece, and I am going to need your full attention.

"I'm not too crazy about . . ."

I've drawn blood on my palms by clenching my fists about this absolute travesty. It's taking everything I've got not to follow each elected official to their lunch break just to replace the tomato on their sandwich with one of those gritty ones that doesn't taste like anything. I will obviously give back the real tomato after that first disappointing bite.

"He/She gets very political on Facebook."

God, I wish they would just shut up. Sometimes they have a point and sometimes they look dumber than a parent fighting with a referee at a first-grade soccer game. Either way, it's just absolutely too much.

"Now, I voted for him/her but . . ."

I also voted for Carrie McKenzie for student council president some time ago, and I didn't invite her to be in our homecoming group because I thought she picked a sh*tty theme. ("Toy Story Under the Stars"? Come on!) She cried in the bathroom at the dance, and I didn't go in to check on her even once. So just because I voted for someone doesn't mean that I'm on their team forever. That reminds me, I should call Carrie and invite her to our Christmas party!

"What do you think about all this . . ."

I have a really strong opinion about it, but I'm going to offer it only if it appears that you agree with me because I don't feel like getting into it today.

"Now I like that [name] girl/fella."

I've seen or read a few things about them, and they appear to make points that I agree with in a demeanor that I generally enjoy. If I ever encounter them in public, I will act like we are old friends even though we have never met.

"Now I gotta be honest, I don't really care for that [name] girl/fella."

I've seen or read a few things about them and find them obnoxious at best and odious at worst. If I ever encounter them in public, I will act like we are old friends even though we have never met.

A NOTE ON
Yard Signs

Less permanent than bumper stickers, more passive than T-shirts, and more aggressive than silence, yard signs are the ultimate Midwestern political discourse. A poster-board sign with a red elephant right across the property line from one with a blue donkey is the heartland's way of saying, "Lookie here. We can disagree and still be neighbors!" Because if there's one thing all Midwesterners can agree on, it's the smug certainty that out of all the US regions, we are the most reasonable.

Many yard signs in the Midwest are erected in support of local candidates who the homeowner knows personally through book club, law school, or "just from around." In most cases, the signs go up during election season and come down as soon as ballots are counted. Think of them as appropriately ephemeral, like holiday decorations or the McRib.

Midwesterners also frequently put up yard signs for nonpolitical purposes, such as those extolling their kids' schools and the names of their favorite extracurricular activities. These do not have to be taken down after Election Day. In fact, many have been known to stick around long, *long* after graduation day.

See how we've already stopped talking about politics even though this is an explainer about political yard signs? That's the Midwestern way. The signs are meant to show support, but they do *not* serve as an invitation to talk politics or otherwise stir controversy. They are merely opinions staked in the ground to be whispered about in the privacy of a neighbor's home.

"How 'bout them [sports team]?"

I'm ready to move on from this subject immediately! Let's laugh about my awkward non sequitur and then quickly resume congratulating each other on our most recent professional or personal successes.

"I think we're done here."

Shut up. Now.

South Dakota

NICKNAME: "The Mount Rushmore State"

REASON: It is the state where Mount Rushmore is.

WHAT EVERYONE THINKS THE CAPITAL IS: "Wait, wait . . . hold on. No, no, I know this. We learned it in school!"

ACTUAL CAPITAL: Pierre

FAMOUS SOUTH DAKOTANS

Bob Barker	January Jones	Sitting Bull (Dakota Territory)
Crazy Horse (Dakota Territory)	Laura Ingalls Wilder	Tom Brokaw

FAMOUS PEOPLE WHO SPENT TIME IN SOUTH DAKOTA, SO IT COUNTS

L. Frank Baum	"Wild Bill" Hickok

Chislic (South Dakota's unofficial state dish)
Here's what it is: Seasoned cubes of deep-fried meat served on a stick.
Any questions?

Mount Rushmore

The Badlands, one of the best places in the world for finding fossils.

South Dakota has more shoreline than Florida!

The Missouri River runs right through the middle of South Dakota, dividing the state into an East and West that are as different culturally as they are geographically. That is to say, significant differences with a lot of common ground. East River is flatland for the farmers with so much corn that they built a palace out of it. West River has the Badlands and the ranches with many more trees and mountains.

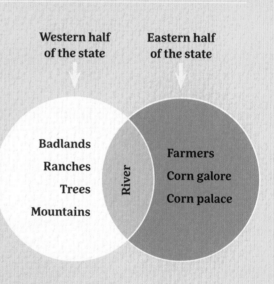

Western half of the state

Eastern half of the state

Badlands
Ranches
Trees
Mountains

River

Farmers
Corn galore
Corn palace

Cyclotrons

"Sue," nickname of one of the most complete and best-preserved tyrannosaurus rex skeletons ever found

Leaving

The Midwestern Goodbye is a social exchange all its own. It lasts anywhere from forty-five minutes to two hours and is instigated by a hearty thigh slap, a bold throaty "Welp!" or, in many cases, both at the same time. What follows is a "you hang up" "no, you hang up" of magnificent proportions—even more if there are additional elements involved, like family members or scheduling the next get-together.

The three components of The Midwestern Goodbye are The Initiation, The Appreciation, and The Anticipation.

The Initiation kicks off the farewell by indicating to all parties that the goodbye is about to commence. It starts with a "*Well, . . .*" or an apology, along with the reason for the departure, whether it's "an early start tomorrow," "getting these kids home to bed," or "some work to finish up before you hit the hay."

Next is The Appreciation, in which everyone discusses how wonderful the past few moments or hours together have been and expresses their joy and relief that "we finally got to do this."

Finally, all Midwesterners close their interaction with The Anticipation. This is the time to make future plans, make plans to make future plans, or to decidedly not make future plans by announcing where everyone will see one another next.

As we say goodbye, Midwesterners always strive to leave with notions of goodwill and warmth all around. To depart each conversation feeling more connected, while also reveling in the prospect of being alone with their thoughts for a little while. After we initiate our parting, appreciate our time together, and anticipate our next meeting, we hem and haw at the exit (real or metaphorical) before offering a loving and final "buh-bye now" as we close the door with a smile and say, to no one but ourselves,

"Well, that was fun, wasn't it."

"Well, it was great talkin' to ya."

I enjoyed this interaction, but I need to end it.

"Well, I'd love to stay and chat, but I gotta run."

I did not enjoy this interaction, and I need to end it.

"I'm so sorry to cut ya off, but I gotta run."

It does not matter whether or not I like you, this interaction happened at the worst possible time, and I am already devastatingly late. I will text you in two hours apologizing for my rudeness.

"I'll see ya around!"

We encountered each other by mistake in a public location and I need to go now. I will make a quick but jovial exit so I can greet the next person I see with "you'll never believe who I just ran into," before waxing eloquent about you.

"Be safe gettin' home, all right?"

I want to communicate well-wishes without committing to another get-together.

"We should do this again sometime."

I had enough fun at this event to suggest a reprise. I will probably not take any action toward a reunion any time soon, but you may take this comment to mean that were you to attempt to plan something else, I would definitely say yes and probably bring dessert!

— or —

I do not mean this. I am merely trying to leave a pleasant thought in your head before I skedaddle the heck out of here. I do not want to see you again. I did not have a good time. If you plan something else and invite me, I will definitely say yes and probably bring dessert.

"I'll tell _____ you said hi!"

I will mention this event to our mutual friend the next time I see them and use it as an excuse to gossip about everything I have learned over the course of this interaction.

"Sorry to interrupt, but we're headin' out."

It honestly took me a good seven minutes to get up the courage to do something so rude as to interrupt your conversation, but I weighed the severity of "interrupting rudeness" against "leaving-without-saying-goodbye rudeness" and there was simply no contest.

"We'd better get goin'."

I have nowhere else to be, but I really don't want to be *here* anymore, and it makes sense to start now since the goodbye will take another forty-five minutes.

"Give _____ a big hug for me."

I want to acknowledge that you are here without a critical member of your inner circle, and I want your [child/spouse/parent] to know that I was thinking about them. You do not have to give them an actual hug. A simple "[my name] sends her love" is fine.

"Let's not go this long without seeing each other again!"

I forgot how much I liked you!

"Lemme walk you guys out!"

Okay, socially unaware heathens, it's time to get the eff out of my house so I can down one more drink and start cleaning up. This isn't my first rodeo, and I know that if I do not physically seal you inside your Honda Accord, your departure could take another two hours and three stories about your trip to Amsterdam seven years ago. We get it! There's a red-light district! You're very adventurous and daring, now please get out of my home. The next time I see cheap flights to Amsterdam, I will forward you the email and suggest we go together.

"Well, I won't keep ya."

We've been talking so long, one of us must have overstayed our welcome by now. I'm concerned that it's me, so I'll take the initiative to draw this to a close so that you perceive me as self-aware. I'll email you tomorrow telling you how great it was to see you.

— or —

I did not want to make this conversation very long at all, but you seem intent on continuing it and I don't want that to happen. I'll bring a six-pack of the beer that you just offhandedly mentioned to our next interaction.

"Well, this was so much fun!"

I have been planning my exit for the past twenty minutes. I will vacate the premises in forty-five minutes once I have said an intimate goodbye to every single person in this room.

"Next time, we'll do it at our place."

I've made a mental note of everything from the quality of the food to the diversity of the company and am now determined to outdo you in every single facet. The first thing I will do when I get home is send you a thank-you text.

— or —

I did not enjoy my time with you or being in your residence. I was one warm glass of Pinot Grigio away from suffocating myself with a HomeGoods bag. I'm hoping that you'll think "the ball is in my court" now and wait an indefinite amount of time before inviting me to another one of these miserable events. The first thing I will do when I get home is send you a thank-you text.

"Well, lemme let you go!"

I was waiting for you to find a graceful way to extract yourself from our interaction, but since you have elected to ignore my body language, codes of human decency, and the entire concept of time itself, I will excuse you *for* you. I have, of course, already paid the check.

"Drive safe."

We've already said goodbye three times and I think this one might be the real thing. I know you have only a fifteen-minute drive home, but I have exhausted all my other parting words. We will say goodbye one more time before you actually leave the premises.

"Buh-bye now."

I am closing the door behind you. This interaction is now officially over.

Wisconsin

NICKNAME: "The Badger State"

REASON

Before it was synonymous with cheese, Wisconsin was known for lead mining. The miners, apparently too busy digging for "gray gold" to build houses, dug makeshift burrows for shelter. These peculiar "badger dens" earned them the nickname "badgers."

WHAT EVERYONE THINKS THE CAPITAL IS: Milwaukee

ACTUAL CAPITAL: Madison

FAMOUS WISCONSINITES

Barbie	Georgia O'Keeffe	Trixie Mattel
Frank Lloyd Wright	Mark Ruffalo	Willem Dafoe
Gene Wilder	Orson Welles	

FAMOUS PEOPLE WHO SPENT TIME IN WISCONSIN, SO IT COUNTS

Harry Houdini	Hattie McDaniel	Oprah

CLAIMS TO FAME

Breweries	Cheese curds	Only publicly owned sports team in the United States

Loyalty to butter

In Wisconsin, it's illegal for a restaurant to serve margarine as a substitute for butter unless the customer specifically orders it. In fact, margarine was totally banned in the state from 1895 to 1967.

YOU CAN THANK WISCONSIN FOR

American Girl dolls **Ice-cream sundaes** **Kindergarten**

Wisconsin Old Fashioned
(brandy > whiskey!)

INGREDIENTS
1 orange slice
2 maraschino cherries
1 sugar cube
2 dashes Angostura bitters
1½ ounces brandy
2 ice cubes

TOPPER OPTIONS
Sweet Lemon-lime soda
Sour Sour mix or grapefruit soda
Press 1 part lemon-lime soda and 1 part club soda
Soda Club soda

GARNISH OPTIONS
Maraschino cherry • Orange slice
Olives • Pickled brussels sprouts
Pickled mushrooms

1
In an old fashioned glass, combine the orange slice, cherries, sugar cube, and bitters and muddle together.

2
Add the brandy to the glass, stir it around a bit, and then add the ice.

3
Top with your choice of soda and garnish as desired.

4
Say *Cheers!* Or *Cheese* is also fine. We are in Wisconsin after all.

A Midwestern Goodbye

Welp, it's about time for me to be heading out. I can't tell you how much fun it's been spending these last one hundred thirty-seven pages together. Hopefully, no matter your native conversation style, this book helped you feel more at home in the heartland or gave you a bit of the heartland to take on home.

There are lots of different ways that Midwesterners say "I love ya." Some make sure the beer's always cold. Some get season tickets to share with the whole neighborhood. Some just pop in for a visit. Some mow the yard next door 'cause they're "already out here, might as well git 'er done." Some drive across the country to celebrate or sympathize. Some scrape the ice off your car. Some pick up the kids from school when mom's stuck at work. Some remember your name after hearing it once. Some bring you a little somethin' for dinner since they know you've got a lot going on right now.

Some write a whole book about how Midwesterners say things. . . .

I can't thank *you* enough for taking the time to join (and finish!) this conversation with me. It's really been somethin' else. I wish I could write each and every one of you a thank-you note, but that's a lot of ink and we all gotta get home in time for the game.

Now, there's no doubt about it, I'm sure I've missed some of your favorite phrases. I'm just one gal. I put my tennis shoes on one at a time just like everyone else. There's no way I got every single Midwestern idiom or quirk in these pages. But hey, do me a favor: Keep me honest by making this guide your own. We've left you a little space here at the end to really do your thing!

Ope! Forgot somethin'? *Put your own favorite Midwestern phrases here!*

_____

_____

_____

_____

_____

_____

_____

_____

Well, I really oughta be going now. I left you a few thank-you notes on the next spread, just in case you want to take some with you. Thanks again for having me. We should do this again sometime. Be safe getting home, okay? I'll be seeing ya real soon.

Don't be a stranger!

Thank-You Notes

Nothing says thank-you for doing a specific Midwestern thing like a thank-you that mentions that specific thing!

Thank you

for helping me bag my leaves.

THANK YOU

for always bringing the dish that I love when we hang out instead of "trying something new."

THANK YOU

for knowing that your yard is way nicer than mine and inviting me over multiple times in a row instead of waiting for me to return the favor.

thank you

for always asking for more chips at restaurants so I don't have to.

THANK YOU

for having other plans every time we go to happy hour, so I never have to figure out when it's appropriate to end the evening.

THANK YOU for leaving your spouse at home every once in a while.

thank you for always letting my child pick a toy out of your prize drawer.

thank you for referring to my junk drawer as a prize drawer.

Thank you for serving alcohol at your child's birthday party.

Thank you for waving to me every morning but only striking up a conversation some mornings.

Thank you for buying me such a great book.

thank you for providing professional services for free because "we're neighbors."

Thank you for reading this book.

Acknowledgments

Gosh dangit, there are so many people who made this book possible. A big Midwestern heck yeah to:

Super-agent Andrea Blatt for speaking my language and being my irreplaceable guide through this entire process.

Sarah Malarkey for being the perfect, compassionate, and brilliant editor and collaborator that I didn't even dare to dream about.

Jovaney Hollingsworth for taking a manuscript and making it into a gorgeous book. You're a genius. I cannot believe how lucky I am to make this with you.

The entire Ten Speed Press Team of Heroes—Stephanie Davis, Mari Gill, Dan Myers, and Claudia Sanchez. Copyeditor Steven Blaski and proofreader Michael Fedison made this book better, and designer Kelly Booth made it beautiful.

Chris Monks for publishing the original piece in *McSweeney's Internet Tendency* and for all the kind rejections before that that kept me going. And Lucy Huber for editing the other pieces in the Midwestern Convo cannon.

Karen Chee, Nicole Tersigni, and Sam Mellinger for reading and supporting my initial proposal.

My teachers, Mark Luce, Bob Kohler, Jerrod Roark, and Lindsay Zimmerman, for giving me the tools, support, and space to become the writer I am today.

Caitlin Kunkel for literally everything. Thank you for helping me build the creative life I've always wanted.

My other Great Week for Women ladies—Kate, Sasha, Brittany, Charu, Emmy, and Casey for being a safe place to fail and to fly.

The St. Nell's Humor Writing Residency and Emily Flake for giving me a beautiful workspace escape that made hitting deadlines in the dead of winter feel homey and romantic and like how writing should feel.

My Midwesterners—Ellen Haun, Kaya LeGrand, Nelly Mueller, Kendall Sherman, Nick Jaroszewicz, Anna Menzel, Jonathan Marks, Jack Elzinga, Steph Warner, and Tessa Wiegand for notes and thoughts and dinners and love.

The rest of the CF crew for always taking my humor seriously.

The Sherman Family for opening your home to me.

My Ayni Brigade team for making this possible; giving me time off to write, providing creative support, and consistently showing humanity and compassion. I am so grateful to you.

Derek Byrne for being the best thing that Missouri ever gave me.

Dad for always telling me that I have something to say.

Tess for always helping me say it the best.

Mom for showing me every single day what it means to put in the work of being creative. And for saying "you have to make this a book" every two weeks for three years until I finally listened. You were right. Again.

Felipe for all of it. Every "quick read" "real fast" before I send this draft in, every cup of coffee, every joke pitch, every "that's great, babe," every bit of this journey was more fun because you were a part of it. I love you.

And Kansas City. I made this for you, thanks for making me.

Published in the United States by Ten Speed Press, an imprint of
Random House, a division of Penguin Random House LLC, New York.
TenSpeed.com
RandomHouseBooks.com

Ten Speed Press and the Ten Speed Press colophon are registered trademarks
of Penguin Random House LLC.

Typefaces: Latinotype's Mohr Rounded, Melvastype's Fineday, FontFont's Marselis

Library of Congress Cataloging-in-Publication Data is on file with the publisher.

Hardcover ISBN: 978-1-9848-6133-7
eBook ISBN: 978-1-9848-6134-4

Printed in China

Editor: Sarah Malarkey
Designer: Kelly Booth | Production designers: Mari Gill and Claudia Sanchez
Production manager: Dan Myers
Copyeditor: Steven Blaski | Proofreader: Michael Fedison
Publicist: David Hawk | Marketer: Stephanie Davis

10 9 8 7 6 5 4 3 2 1

First Edition